The Art of the Smart

NEAL J HORWITZ

The Art of the Smart

Smart

How to steer your career

NEAL J HORWITZ

DISCLAIMER

This book is licensed for your personal enjoyment and education only. While best efforts have been used, the author and publisher are not offering legal, accounting, medical, or any other professional services advice and make no representations or warranties of any kind and assume no liabilities of any kind with respect to the accuracy or completeness of the contents and specifically disclaim any implied warranties of merchantability or fitness of use for a particular purpose, nor shall they be held liable or responsible to any person or entity with respect to any loss or incidental or consequential damages caused, or alleged to have been caused, directly or indirectly, by the information or programs contained herein. Stories, characters, and entities are fictional. Any likeness to actual persons, either living or dead, is strictly coincidental.

The information contained in this ebook is current at the time of this writing. Although all attempts have been made to verify the information provided in this publication, neither the author nor the publisher assumes any responsibility for errors, omissions, or contrary interpretations of the subject matter herein.

The views expressed are those of the author alone, and should not be taken as expert instruction or commands. The reader is responsible for his or her own actions. Adherence to all applicable laws and regulations, including international, federal, state, and local governing professional licensing, business practices, advertising, and all other aspects of doing business is the sole responsibility of the purchaser or reader. Neither the author nor the publisher assumes any responsibility or liability whatsoever on the behalf of the purchaser or reader of these materials.

CONTENTS

To Jane, n*unc scio quid sit amor*

PART 1: GETTING HIRED

INTRODUCTION: THE SONG IS YOU

You've likely heard it before, but it bears repeating: When looking for an executive position, know how to talk about yourself with poise.

I find many executives tongue-tied when saying out loud—in an interview setting—what their strengths are. Nothing unusual about that; we seldom spout off about our genius to those we don't know, nor to colleagues with a 'look how good I am' monologue (I'm skipping over the chest-beating churls who never miss a chance to preen).

However, when you decide to *actively* scope the market, you're evaluated on the complete package:

- Do you have the presentation and appearance, which fits into a particular work environment?
- How is your 'elevator pitch'?
- Have you written nicely honed curriculum vitae (CV) that highlights your strengths?
- Can you clearly articulate your values? (This, by the way, takes some rehearsing before going on stage.)

If you have *not* actively looked for a new position in some time, you must now relearn the basic one-two, cha-cha-cha—the rhythm of the job hunt.

Think hard about *you*—your core strengths (which you might shrug off), your know-how, and where you are consistently asked to help because you make a *difference*.

Still not sure? Ask those who know you for a quick, detached assessment. Someone commented to me recently that LinkedIn endorsements actually do create a reasonably good facsimile of what you're known for, the truest way of others seeing your skills as you may not see yourself.

We all have talent to offer. Self-help books the world over have page after page of the same chipper clichés: 'Find your strengths', 'Follow your dreams', 'Decide what you want', 'You too can choose to live your life'. But these worn mantras are repeated because we too often deny or bury our true strengths.

You have unique skills—a song that is only you. (By the way, the title of this introduction, 'The Song Is You', is a 1930s classic composed by Jerome Kern and written by Oscar Hammerstein, which sweetly states that *you* are the words and music that make the song.) You know what jazzes you and where you shine. If not, get moving and find out. You are judged on action only, not hopes and wishes (though those are a start).

We are what we do, not what we think, so know yourself well enough *through* your actions, and sing your song—again and again—until your voice is pleasing to the ear.

1

THE CV IS ALIVE AND WELL, THANK YOU

I look at CV's every day, which allows me to know how a well-written one should read. For various reasons, people usually despise writing their CV, yet most are in need of repair.

One friend splashed his thoughts down on a rewritten CV and trotted over to a headhunter acquaintance of his (for the record, I'm an *über* headhunter). The headhunter did a quick 'face-lift' (likely some touch-ups), and my friend waltzed out of the office, thinking it was completed. As headhunters are wont to do, he also told my friend there were three jobs he could probably get him in the door.

In recounting all this, he asked if it was alright to send me his reworked CV. Sure, why not, I replied. He emailed it over, and the face-lift had not taken. I [politely] ripped it apart and delved into the details; typos, syntax, measurements, profitability to philanthropy, the 'And what was the result'? Questions—lots of red ink and many edits. I didn't do so to irritate my friend, but to force him to think about his achievements, distil them to bite-sized points, see his patterns of success more clearly, and market himself more confidently.

I don't do face-lifts. It was a counselling session through a CV. It often is.

He took my edits under counsel, and, because he's a smart guy, listened to and thanked me for opening his eyes to doing what he should have done a while ago. He got it.

During another typical week, four people asked for help with their CV's. All of them had about twenty-five years of work experience; all extremely smart and polished. None had updated their CV in years, and each was hesitant about where to start—asking about length, format, content, and buzzwords to put in or avoid. All had a *cri de coeur* of 'Aaarrggh, I hate this' angst.

The CV is an important reflection of who we are. It is *not* outdated media. I read articles which state it's an anachronism, not needed in our day of social media. Online profiles are more easily updated, interactive, and not as linear or limiting as a CV, which misses the point. Your CV is not a LinkedIn profile, blog post, or Facebook page. How can it be? It's your personal track record of success.

The CV is a necessity. Accept it. And it *should* be a bit of a struggle to do well. It is a personal opus, written with brevity. It allows the reader to skim—not read—and be able to clearly discern your strengths, a personal haiku, if you will. What could be easier than that? After all, we spend inordinate amounts of time online, often burnishing our profiles. A CV should be a walk in the park, but most of us cannot fathom rewriting or updating it with compelling points.

Working on your CV should be an engaging process of introspection. The benefit of grappling (only for a few hours at most) with your CV is that it forces you to confront yourself. Writing about your work is to face who you are. Anyone who thinks such introspection is easy has never done it properly, but doing something well takes time and dedication.

I have often found that those requiring the most help are senior-level individuals—understandable, as many executives have used their internal network, rather than a CV, to move upward. A strong and well-balanced CV is an accurate reflection of strengths, achievements, patterns, and interests—that's not bad ammunition to have close by, is it?

If taken to heart, you come out on the other side of the writing process with more assurance to take on the world with a strong personal marketing tool.

The CV matters now, and, as long as there continues to be work, it will stay with us well into the future.

Elements of the Well-Crafted CV

Have I convinced you? Want to get to work? Here are some essential elements of a well-crafted CV:

A well-ordered CV will show a pattern of YOU

This is not an unbroken one, but a pattern of success and adversity. It lets you do what many of us instinctively veer from: self-reflection and self-promotion. The CV gives license to politely brag—not the 'Hey, Ma, look at me' sort of sleeve tugging—but to list things you have managed, grown, saved, contributed, streamlined, created, negotiated, influenced, operated, or blown up. Think and write down your strengths, then try it on for size—all such reflection is important.

Once someone sent me a CV, forewarning it was 'primitive'. It was, and outdated by two years, something I call the 'layer cake' CV, adding on to the top but never looking at the layers below. You end up with a rat's nest, not a snapshot of accomplishments. How do you view yourself? Would you hire you?

Brand yourself

A well-crafted CV allows branding. Think about past accomplishments that mattered: achievements recognised and rewarded; projects measured monetarily or collaboratively; groups managed, built, or cut; influencing or lobbying with results; dealing with adversity and weak markets, and so on. What are the strengths and skill sets you're known for? Equally important, what *do* you want to be known for?

Show your strengths

A CV must highlight what one does well, clearly, concisely, and confidently—listing two points will more than suffice. What you *do* have a gift for must be accentuated and repeated. People hire on strength, never weakness. A well-written CV allows you to politely stretch and strut.

Interesting interests, please

Under 'Interests' there should be something beyond the lukewarm line of 'reading, hiking, travelling, seeing the world, and music'.

This section is important because it distinguishes the person as having a passion, another type of innate intelligence and curiosity.

Let me present two business luminaries to reinforce why 'interests' matter and how these two interview candidates.

First is Bing Gordon, now partner with VC (venture capital) firm Kleiner Perkins Caufield & Byers, who states:

> *'In hiring . . . I will always ask about your learning practices, who are your heroes, what do you read. I want to know your hobbies, what's the personal arc you see for your career, where are you trying to get to'.*

Gordon goes on to say he reads résumés upside down and starts with personal interests. If somebody doesn't have believable interests, and if they aren't passionate about something in life, they're not going to be able to bring it. *'What have you done that's any good'?* Gordon likes to ask. *'And strip out all the history stuff; just tell me what you're proud of and how you think about it'.*[1]

Second is Robert Iger, Disney's CEO, who says:

> *'[In hiring someone] getting to know them, getting under their skin to the extent possible, becomes important . . . I love curiosity, particularly in our business—being curious about the world, but also being curious about your business, new business models, new technology'.*

---

[1] Adam Bryant, 'Power? Thanks, but I'd Rather Have Influence', *The New York Times*, June 4, 2011, http://www.nytimes.com/.

Iger goes on to say that he tries to learn more about a person, what the candidate does outside of work, his family, what his interests are, what they are passionate about because 'Passion suggests some level of curiosity'.[2]

One caveat: The above quotes can easily be read within a Western framework, and some senior Asian talent might be less likely to reflect on outside interests. But this is the age of the global firm, and everyone at a senior level must understand how to communicate their values and character on levels far beyond the realm of functional. No company hires at a top level based on function alone. Work is grounded in character. At work, character is charted by values, energy, and integrity—all of which are easily reflected in 'Interests'.

Also disregard any nonsense you may have heard regarding writing a CV in order for search engines to 'see' enough relevant words. A robotic CV will not get you a senior-level job.

If you're planning on working for a robot, I suggest you review this CNBC article.[3]

Read it for laughs, which may be the point anyhow. Then get back to the work of good clear writing, safe in the comfort of what you're strong at, and knowing where you (likely) want to go in your career. That's plenty.

By the way, no one yet has asked me to help with their LinkedIn profile. And they shouldn't; it's not the same thing at all.

Don't Forget: It's about Who You Know

With my focus on the importance of the CV, I would be remiss if I failed to mention an issue highlighted in the *Wall Street Journal*. The issue is regarding the woes of job hunters who answer job adverts online or from websites, and the overwhelmed in-house talent acquisition people who seldom respond. Applicants keep sending CV's, wondering if the jobs even

---

[2] Adam Bryant, 'He Was Promotable, After All', *The New York Times*, May 2, 2009, http://www.nytimes.com/.

[3] Cindy Perman, 'The Killer Resume: How to Get Hired by the Machines', *CNBC*, March 22, 2012, http://www.cnbc.com/id/46823506.

exist, waiting for a reply of any kind, pumping away and assuming the numbers game will pay off at some point.

Does any of this sound familiar to you? If it does, STOP! You won't get anywhere by answering anything online. Yes, I know, LinkedIn has become a better place for job seekers and employers to find one another, and no doubt there will be more user-friendly online sites for job seekers and recruiters in the future. That's the way of the world, and the good news is it will put some of the more unctuous recruiting companies out of business. Good riddance.

Buried in the *Wall Street Journal* article is a jewel about how to get ahead. 'Experts say . . . the single best method of getting a job remains a referral from a company employee'.[4]

That's right. Stating the obvious, the secret sauce has not changed in decades, regardless of email and online communication. *It's who you know, and who talks about you.* You want to get noticed? Get yourself in someone's face, real or virtual, work on increasing your profile more than your CV (once your CV is spot on, that is). Many jobs are indeed gotten when some-one in the company turns to someone else and asks, 'Know anyone good'? That's the way the world goes 'round.

If you want that job, or promotion, start with getting (positively) no-ticed, step number one. The CV matters, but not a bit if all you do is send it out with a hope and a prayer. Work on standing out, having a point of view, and being proud of your achievements. Then you'll be ready for the next step.

---

[4] Lauren Weber, 'Your Résumé vs. Oblivion', *The Wall Street Journal: Asia Edition*, January 24, 2012, http://online.wsj.com/asia.

2

A BRIEF HUNTING *GUIDE* FOR JOB SEEKERS

So now you've written a CV that made sense—not too long, not too short, and something succinct. What's next?

Use your time to search for the *right* job. While I advocate raising your profile, don't squander your time attending as many interviews as possible. People often panic when looking for a new job. This creates a mindset of fear, and when fearful, one grabs the first thing that comes along, which often results with the wrong job, unhappy soon after, underperforming, and doomed to repeat their job search over and over again. But it does not have to be that way—there are ways to find a job that fits.

Thousands of books on interviewing techniques and how to land a perfect job have already been written. Many people think if they do their research, scrutinize the classifieds, brush up their CV, learn how to answer standard interview questions, dress well, and get through the first interview in one piece, they are on their way to job happiness.

Nothing could be further from the truth. The focus should not be on how to *get* a job, but on how to *do* a job.

My friend, Brian, is a good case in point. He lived overseas, in three different countries in Asia, for more than fifteen years. Laid off from his last US-based organisation, with a wife and children to support, he was given outplacement help from a large firm in Singapore: an 'office', a computer, a psychometric exam, some pointers on his CV, a few interview tips, a pat on his behind, and off he went.

He spent his days calling every headhunter and agency listed, reviewing online recruitment sites and job boards, and sending out several CV's each week. When we talked about his travails, he'd had four interviews so far and was debating taking on a new job.

Brian didn't trust his new boss-to-be, thought he'd be a micromanager, wasn't sure if the company goals set for him were realistic, the pay/bonus scheme made him think it might not be a sound company, and couldn't figure out how the company seemingly made its numbers.

The company had a nice office, was interested in him, and he needed a job—why not grab it and make some money?

Here's why not. Many people such as Brian attend interviews, but know little about the company, the job, or any of the organisational issues. Their information is limited to what they have read in the company brochure or on the website. If your boss asked you to spearhead a new strategic initiative, would you wait for him to explain everything or would you instead find out as much as possible prior to your meeting? You'd likely do the latter—or should. How can someone with little background knowledge on a company be able to talk about corporate challenges during an interview?

Always view an interview as an opportunity to show what you can do for your 'new' boss. *Act like an employee*, not an interviewee. Your goal is to get the right job for you. If you are a mid- to senior-level professional, you know that there are *not* hundreds, or even dozens, of jobs that are the right ones for you.

As a headhunter, I get calls and email messages from people asking if I can help them get more interviews and get in front of as many companies as possible, running from one interview to the next to see which is a better fit.

Maybe you have become like Brian—good at interviewing, going online every day, sending CV's out scattershot (almost all of which never see the light of day), and being interviewed at every possible opportunity. That is busy work, not progress.

People assume they have to get plenty of rejections before they get that dream job. They continue trying for jobs they *know* are not right; hoping somehow one of these mismatched interviews will blossom into the ideal career. CV after CV is sent out, and it keeps an entire industry of in-house recruiters, online job boards, and employment agencies busy.

Going for interviews, however, is not your job. Your job is to size up the opportunity given to you.

Before you think about going for the next interview, do your homework on the company and the job itself. Ask yourself if it is a good fit, given your skills and interests. If it isn't, don't try to ace the interview for its own sake and end up leaving an important career decision to the wrong person—the interviewer.

Use the time you would have spent preparing and going for the interview on pointed activities to help you achieve better results and candidacy for the *right* job.

Some Pointers on the Hunt

As you sail forth, keep in mind the following:

Do not rely exclusively on headhunters. In one week I had coffee with five people looking for opportunities, all saying how many headhunters they knew. I told them all to stop it. Headhunters will seldom get them a job; it's a secondary, maybe tertiary source. And you know what? They all agreed!

Get off your ass. Social media is great, perfect for research, but get into the agora as often as possible, build your profile, refine your pitch. Actors and salespeople say the same thing over again until it sounds natural. So should you.

Be comfortable talking about you. Be proud of what you've done and who you are; we all have a compelling story to tell. If you don't toot your horn, no one hears the music.

Nosce te ipsum, **know yourself.** When George Hu, Salesforce's chief operating officer (COO), was asked about what career advice he'd like to give, he said,

'Really know yourself well. A question I ask people in interviews is, "How would you describe who you are, in the core of your DNA, in one word?" People often struggle with that [question]. The most common response I get is, "Do you really mean one word?" So know who you are, and really understand what you're exceptional at'.[5]

We are all known for something we do better than others—most of the time. If you're *really* not sure, ask others who know you and can give objective input.

Be proud of *what* you're good at. Do not harp on what you are not good at; no one has yet been hired on weaknesses.

Most of you have many interests, but only a couple of true strengths from which you'll make your mark. That doesn't guarantee you'll get the job, but it does provide assurance of being clearer on where you'll likely fit.

Be aware of language differences. Hiring managers lean towards their own kind, assuming they'll understand each other and 'speak the same language'.

Not long ago I had breakfast in Beijing with a friend, a mainland Chinese in real estate who'd gone to grad school in the United States. He recalled an interview he'd had three years ago with a US-based private equity firm.

'They called me up, I think it was one of the [American] directors, and we had a good talk on joining them. Towards the end of the call, he asked me if I thought I was a "superstar". I thought that was a bit odd, as I'd never thought of myself as a "superstar", which I'd usually reserve for the very, very top of any group. Anyhow I told him I was good, capable, reliable, and we left it at that, as there were more interviews they'd arranged. I'm Chinese, you know? We don't boast about being the "greatest", we're not brought up that way. As a Chinese, it is about being humble and not bragging. Anyhow, I never got the job, and I found out the chairman had put the word out he wanted a "superstar" in China, and that was all they

---

[5]   Adam Bryant, 'Using Just One Word, Try to Describe Your Career DNA', *The New York Times*, April 18, 2013, http://www.nytimes.com/.

cared about. I still think about it, as that would have been a great job, and I won't make that same mistake again'.

This can also apply in reverse, a Westerner in an Asian company. Be aware of language and its subtleties that vary from place to place.

Map out your plan—for your eyes only. Never say, "If you hear of something let me know." Be targeted, be direct. Know your audience before you meet, try to leave every conversation—real or virtual—with a lead or door opener. Make your spreadsheet of A, B, and C targets, by company, by industry, and by contact. It is a living document and constantly changes.

Your best friends are not your best contacts. Contacts one or two degrees removed are those who assess you on skills, not friendship. They're the ones you need to grab.

Build your own 'advisory board', a handful of people—former bosses, colleagues, ex-clients, all who know your character and strengths. Use them as a sounding board when needed. And you will. It all comes around anyhow, and they'll rely on you for something at some point.

Be grateful. My friend Mike reminded me of this recently. Mike is a senior C-level executive,[6] and regularly writes for five minutes (writes—not thinks) a day a short list of what he is grateful for. Do it long enough and it becomes habit.

Interview Warning Signs

You've done your research and found a company that outwardly appears to be the right fit. The interview seemed to have gone well, but did it? There are telltale signs during an interview that can warn you something is amiss. Here are four clues to possibly larger issues.

1. The interviewer keeps you waiting more than 30–40 minutes. It does not matter how busy he or she is; you're busy too—we all are.

---

[6] Executives at the chief level. CCO, CEO, CFO, etc.

Lateness on the part of the interviewer is a warning of poor time management or disregard for being an interviewer.

2. Little preparation has been made. The interviewer has not reviewed your CV or the job brief, and it is clear the interview process is a burden to be hurried through, rather than an opportunity to meet a new candidate.

3. The interviewer cannot answer much about the role, or is ill-informed or cavalier about the scope, measurements, or potential of the position.

4. The interviewer does most of the talking—few questions are asked, and those asked are superficial, and the time may be cut short. No insight given, none exchanged, nothing marketed.

3

ONBOARDING VS. WATERBOARDING: SIMPLE RULES OF HOW NOT TO DROWN AT THE OUTSET

'Onboarding? More like waterboarding', said a friend to me when I asked him if his new company was onboarding him at all. I later met up with someone else who said the new company's onboarding strategy was to go around the office and introduce the COO, CMO, CIO (who said 'Don't bother me, just go to global headquarters'.) and that was it—and for a fairly senior level hire.

Surprising as it is in the day of strategic HR and all the blather of 'war for talent', the best way to onboard, as is true in life, is to do it yourself if you want it done well.

A new job is fraught with expectations from the new hire and the hiring company. The onboarding process should allow a new person to move into the new role more smoothly during the first few months. Companies are now refining their onboarding from fairly useless (does anyone remember 'orientation'?) to more strategic and helpful. The truth is that many companies and leaders still do a subpar job, saying to the new hire, 'Now that you're here, you'll figure it out, you're a smart operator—and we definitely do not want it done the way it was before. Over to you'.

I'm overdramatising it to make a point. Some bosses claim to be far, far too busy and travel too often to have more than a couple of meetings with their new hire in the first few weeks. As I just stated, it is incumbent on the new hire to do his or her own on boarding. The truth is that's perfectly good. Preferable, in fact.

Once inside a new company, time is best spent understanding the rhythm and pace, reading the room, building alliances, and learning precedence. It is NOT rolling your sleeves up and 'getting into the job', certainly not if you're at a senior level.

No one can succeed—no matter how smart and enthusiastic they are—if they are not liked or respected in a new company. No one. They will either be pushed out, or leave in a huff, muttering about what a difficult place it was to get anything done.

Here then is some onboarding advice for senior executives:

Do

Do learn how to communicate with senior management while developing your own style of leadership within your new surroundings.

Do know how to deal with less visible rivals and predecessors—accept life as it is.

Do impart confidence and knowledge to others close by as often as possible.

Do pace yourself and do not be seen as a worker bee always at the office.

Do take time to determine your predecessor's legacy, good or bad; both are necessary in order to do your job.

Don't

Don't spend an inordinate amount of time on the job function, but do spend time in developing key relationships.

Don't take too long to get your bearings straight—the honeymoon is getting shorter and shorter.

Don't accept hazy expectations from top management—get clarity.

Don't accept too many tasks at once—that's being a worker bee and not achievable.

Don't try to go it alone and ignore resources close by.

Onboarding is serious stuff, and management needs to understand that. But until that happens, do it yourself (DIY) is the best—and sanest—recourse.

If you can't figure out the job, you're either in over your head, you jumped too fast, or you're in a nightmarish organisation—or all of the above. It happens. If so, get help to see how to salvage it, as it can be remedied most of the time. Many executives ironically think what succeeded at the last place will work at the new place. Half the time they're wrong.

Confused by your new job? Get a coach, get some help, but *don't* deny the problem by working harder and hoping it will go away. Companies often do not think through what a (new) role is supposed to achieve. Jobs are often ill-defined, nor measured to last. For most new C-level hires, it is 70 percent political awareness, alliances, and behaviour, with only 30 percent of the job focusing on function. The higher up you go, the more you are judged by behaviour, not hours worked, which brings me to my next point:

Tortoise-and-Hare Management Lesson

Do not martyr yourself and die on the job. I know plenty of people who have a distinct work modus operandi; I see it on their CV's, reinforced when we meet. They take a new position, determined to show everyone how well they can do—no, how much *better* than anyone else they can do the job. Off to the races they go. Loads of travel, loads of meetings, offsites, constant emails, proposals, conference calls, nonstop, and on-the-go. Twelve, eighteen, or twenty-four months later, they indeed have done the job of three people, or completed a task that should have taken triple the time. Ta-da!!

They're exhausted, but have a satisfied 'I told you I'd do it better and faster' air. Ironically, many times they lament of not knowing what to do next. They've worked themselves out of a job, and maybe it's time to move on—management doesn't appreciate their hard work and travel anyhow. With all their travel they're out of the loop at headquarters (HQ), hadn't spent any time building their contacts. Their health and family have both suffered. The one thing they can rightfully claim is how quickly that mountain of work was scaled.

We all know it's not a 100-yard dash, not even a marathon. Our work life goes on a long, long time, hopefully at a steadier pace than not. There will always be business goals to meet. That will never change. Don't burn out on a new job by racing up a mountain to plant the flag at the top; you'll only be asked to run up another one.

Steady is better, I assure you. Use your time to better know the people within the organisation; build your network and dialogue. That's more valuable than racing to catch that flight, secure in the knowledge that everyone knows how damned hard you work.

And if you're reading this, thinking, *'But my boss does that too! Hell, we all work like that'*, have a good long talk with yourself about what you want from your life and career.

Careers Finished by a Few Sentences

A word of caution before going further.

I had dinner recently with the senior vice president (SVP) of Asia for a US-based company. During the course of the evening, he referred to one person who'd been at the company fifteen years, recently promoted, but whom the SVP felt would not make it. In his words: *'He doesn't have the right sense of urgency'*. He then commented on a new hire who reported directly in to him: *'Good guy, but I watched him in some meetings, and I'm not sure he's a quick enough study. Might not have been a good hire, but we'll see'*. Another direct report, ethnic Chinese with very good spoken English, but the SVP wants English fluency, especially when giving PowerPoints and presentations, no mistakes, no typos: *'He's a smart guy, but if he doesn't double-check his spelling, what does that tell me about how careful he is in the business'*?

He's not about to fire any of them, but he's watching. It's likely none of them know what's being said about them—by him, or anyone else within the company. The first person is too busy trying to manage his business day-to-day, the second one just started and is determining how to fit in, and the third probably thinks his English is fine the way it is, with no need to improve.

Their careers can be derailed, in part because they're not spending enough time building their relationships and reputations, but instead working harder to show the boss how good a job they can do. The boss is not watching them operationally, but strategically, and evaluating how well they click with staff, with peers, with clients.

Moral of the story: focus on what's going on around you, not just the job. Anyone high up in the ranks can tell you that. If you're headed upward, keep your eyes and ears open all the time. You'll be amazed at what can be heard and seen.

PART 2: WORKPLACE CODE OF CONDUCT

4

GAME RULES

Most of us try our best at work—for ourselves, our colleagues, bosses, and clients. Within the workplace there are general rules of the game—a code of conduct—which helps ensure correct behaviour. When those rules are severely bent or broken—by you or by others—attitudes may darken. It's a good time to sit on the bench and let the game play out. This chapter outlines general advice on healthy workplace attitudes and practices, but first—my thoughts from the trenches for a code of conduct at work:

Do not purposely hurt or impugn others, overtly or subtly. It's damage either way; you'll be labeled 'trouble', and it's the surest way to get thrown out of the game.

Watch what comes out of your mouth and what you write; it will come back and bite you; learn to be mute when needed; store the vituperative emails for twenty-four hours, then stir and edit.

Have a firm ethical and moral compass to follow at all times. Don't deviate—otherwise you'll never sleep well.

Give away your knowledge and skills to those who can use it. Selfishness gets you benched.

Always remember you have unique skills and strengths. Work those particular muscles until there's a bulge—it takes practice to look or sound natural.

Skip the envy, jealousy, and sniping of others. Stop comparing upwards or sideways. Learn to be comfortable in your own skin—it fits you perfectly.

Don't get nervous when handed the ball. Practice your self-talk and self-imagery of inner strength. Know what you're going to say and how you're going to act. Yes, talking to yourself absolutely has merit.

Sometimes we're lucky and sometimes it's hard work; the two are not the same, but both are ingredients for success. Understand which is which before you congratulate yourself or others.

Never assume everyone plays the game by your rules; many play by their own rules. Don't get agitated, but recognise their game when you see it and decide if it's worth joining or not.

Listen and watch the A-players carefully—they're stars for a reason. Pick and choose what they do that works for you. We all succeed on the shoulders of others. Study and learn; it's never too late.

Don't ramble or hog the ball. No one has time to watch showboating or listen to slender rhetoric. Be interesting, be engaging, and politely and accurately pass the ball consistently.

Be an adept and facile communicator; written, verbal, physical, and aural. Having 'presence' uses all those skills.

Make no decision or judgment when angry. Communicating when agitated is a sure-fire way to show others you are off balance; the only impact made will be on your side of the bench.

No tantrums allowed. Don't like something? Be counterintuitive. Not everyone will agree or listen, but don't scream. That's a red flag, and the game is finished, whether you're the boss or not. A glare—or silence—is often sufficient. But words spoken hastily and venomously get you nowhere.

Often attributed to the philosopher Philo, 'Be kind, as everyone you meet is carrying a heavy burden'. You never know what is going on in someone else's life, nor should you. Kindness lasts, and it is what we humans are supposed to be.

This code of conduct goes hand-in-hand with the following section.

Don't Be a Smart-Ass at Work

My strong advice to those entering the work force, as well as a reminder for those work veterans: Don't be a smart-ass. Here's what smart-asses do on the job:

Do not take instructions well. Work is about doing what you're told—*the way the boss or the company wants it done.* If you want to do it differently, build it over time, steadily, not at the outset. Or leave and do it on your own.

Act dismissively and all-knowing. I can think of few things that drive a boss to despair more than a new young hire who—verbally and physically—says 'Yeah, yeah, I get it already, whatever', with a verbal and slangy wave of the hand and knack of appearing disengaged when instructions are set. The smart-ass often lacks politesse.

Have bad body language. Similar to dismissiveness, this includes lack of eye contact (or worse, rolling one's eyes), combined with a look of either perplexion or irritation at being disturbed. Some people have no idea how they appear when listening to others. If you furrow your brow a lot, mouth silently to yourself 'Easy, big cheese'—your lips will turn into a smile with no effort. Really.

Use sarcasm. Being bitey, mocking, or sarcastic is a sign of insecurity or attention-getting. A smart-ass uses words as a weapon, freely and caustically, which is a bad habit to fall into. Don't do it. Ever. I used to imitate my peers and bosses (I'm a pretty good mime) and would do so with great frequency and gusto. Anyone care to know if it helped my career?

Don't know how to get along. Years ago I had a really difficult boss, but we respected each other and got along most of the time.

There was an offsite meeting at a hotel with the entire office and some of the big brass was in town to make a presentation. My boss told me to sit in front at his table or close by, as he said I needed the visibility. I was too much of a punk and a contrarian to listen, paid scant interest in toeing the company line, and thought the offsite was silly. I got to the meeting late and sat in the back of the room with the rowdy crowd, not where I was supposed to be. He grabbed me afterward and asked what the hell I was doing, that he was trying to help me, and so on.

Take it from a former smart-ass expert; do *not* do what I did. It fails every single time, guaranteed.

It's Not All about You

One bit of coaching advice I often give C-level execs is, 'It's not all about you', which I find myself also saying to my children . . .

Let me explain. The word I dance with is 'humility', which I'll simply define as 'understanding not everything that happens for the better is because of your effort and genius'.

Your professional or personal life may turn out quite well, but it is not all due to your pedigree or insight. Conversely, some things may have failed or come up short, but not solely because you're slow on the uptake.

We all start out as newborns when the world in fact *does* revolve around us. We cry and yell, and we're appeased. The infant grows, and the stages start of sharing, waiting, and cooperating, which is the give and take of life. Some of us, however, never quite leave that infantile stage. Some become adults who take the credit when it's not theirs to take, do not listen well nor reciprocate or give back. They're the bosses who make unrealistic demands and use staff for personal preening,[7] the parents who berate their children, they insist on winning every argument and debate at all emotive cost; they are the intolerant and dismissive crowd.

The antithesis are those who think everything is their fault; company earnings go down, their team loses a large client, or their child flunks classes or cannot get into the right college. Exhausting as that is, some people get satisfaction from being the perpetual victim and perceived culprit.

Life, work, parenting, relationships . . . none of it is 'fair', but the possibilities are limitless once you accept it as it is, not as it should ideally

---

[7] For a terrific and insane example, look at the Abercrombie & Fitch CEO's corporate jet manual: http://www.thesmokinggun.com/documents/Abercrombie-Fitch-gulfstream-rules-687452.

be. A wise rabbi phrased it well: '*To expect the world to treat you fairly because you're an honest person is like expecting a bull not to charge you because you're a vegetarian*'.

Many of the things that happen to us, good or bad, are seldom highly important or unusually dramatic (although my teenagers would beg to differ). The big issues are thankfully few and far between. Most challenges are not life-threatening, and most successes are not newsworthy.

Humility lets you know that *some* of what happens *is* under your control, the difference between a setback and a tragedy, a step forward or a smashing triumph.

Something didn't go your way? Part of it may be you; part of it was beyond your control. Something good happen? Terrific, as some of it was your effort, and some may have been other factors. It's not all about you.[8]

Who Trusts Ya, Baby

David H. Maister wrote a book years ago, *The Trusted Advisor*, targeted at consultants wishing to forge stronger relationships with clients. The issue of trust swirls around the workplace constantly. How do we work with one another across regions, cultures, and silos if we're unsure of others' capabilities, efforts, or worthiness; how do we trust one another?

As Maister noted, trust is like ballroom dancing, if it is going to work, one leads and one follows. There must be one person trusting, and the other person must be trusted or you can't even dance two steps.

Some of Maister's 'trust' checklist is applicable within the business organisation. Think about these in relation to how you work with your superior, or, conversely, how you manage your team:

---

[8] Special thanks to Harold Kushner, as this was the name of a chapter in his book *Overcoming Life's Disappointments*.

The more you are trusted, the more others will:

- Reach for your advice
- Allow you to be comfortable
- Be inclined to accept your recommendations
- Give you the benefit of the doubt
- Bring you in on more advanced, complex and strategic issues
- Share more information that helps you help them
- Involve you early on when their issues begin to form and take shape
- [Introduce] you to their friends and business acquaintances
- Lower the level of stress in your interactions
- Give you the benefit of the doubt
- Protect you when you need it
- Warn you of dangers you might avoid[9]

Where are you on this list when it comes to your interactions at work? How are you viewed, understood, respected, listened to?

As always said, trust must be gained and is not simply given. Evaluate yourself next to the above checklist on where you might be on that trust scale.

Career Coaching, Swish, Kobe and the Changing Game Plan

Here are my career coaching thoughts on the changing game plan.

I read an article dissecting the dysfunction of the Los Angeles Lakers; how they couldn't play as a team, coaches came and went, a funk they couldn't shake. Amid this, Kobe Bryant changed from his usual role to dishing out more assists than points. The article quoted him when asked how he and the team were evolving and trying to get back on track.

---

[9] David H. Maister, Charles H. Green, and Robert M. Galford, *The Trusted Advisor* (New York: Touchstone, 2000).

'I was probably born a scorer, but I was made a winner', Bryant told reporters. *'Whatever works, whatever wins championships, whatever wins games, that's what I do'.*[10]

We all know shooters don't win; teams do. Bryant may well have been born with one type of talent. But it was only after repeated work, over and over and over again that he came to understand he wanted to win more than to score—not a natural tendency among athletes or executives.

Being forced out of your comfort zone to take on things you thought were well beyond you is daunting, but often well worth the uncertainty. It's a more mature outlook, not the 'me, me, over here!' yelp, and it takes looking towards the horizon, pacing yourself accordingly, contributing wherever you can help to win.

Here are some thoughts to consider for your own coaching.

How many of you:

- Know how to change from your usual role to another related one, continuing to warrant the same level of respect and trust?
- Are comfortable taking centre stage and equally comfortable in a supporting role?
- Can step up and take control of the power that's rightfully yours, even if others are not used to it?
- Diplomatically let others know exactly what you're contributing and how you're doing it?
- Are able to manage your teammates and boss (or coach!) well enough to get results?
- Get those results collaboratively and enjoyably, the way the boss and coach want it done?
- Are liked and respected at work?

---

[10] Howard Beck, 'Lakers Are Again a Changed Team', *The New York Times*, February 4, 2013, http://www.nytimes.com.

The Mechanics of Manners: Ten Points

My children were on school break last week, doing the things teens do: hanging with friends, sleeping late, social media, Skype, videos, and sleepovers.

My son had two of his friends spend the night, and they were up until 2 A.M. When they finally headed out the following afternoon, one of the boys said, 'Thanks for having me over, Mr. Horwitz'. 'Sure', I replied, 'Anytime'. The other boy said nothing, and I thought little of it, as most teenage boys grunt, rather than talk to an adult unless forced.

That evening, the first boy called our home, asking for my son who was not in, then asked to speak to me. He then thanked me again for having him over. I again said I was happy to have had him over, no problem. A couple of sentences, and that was the extent of our conversation. I thought, *Well-mannered kid*, and caught myself juxtaposing him with the other boy, but in the other boy's defence I thought, *Not a big deal, teens are teens*.

And yet, here I am writing about it because it *does* matter. Manners can be called the 'instruction booklet' for humans. No one is born with innate manners; you have to be told how to behave, and learn how from repetition, as is true with anything worth doing well. Manners are the foundation for a civil society. More than even the rule of law, manners get people to cooperate, listen, and behave well.

Emily Post's definition: 'Manners are a sensitive awareness of the feelings of others. If you have that awareness, you have good manners, no matter what fork you use'.

Here are my ten points for day-to-day manners.

Good manners are when you:

1. Can put up with those who lack them.
2. Understand the difference between compliments and flattery, and understand how to deliver the former and avoid the latter.
3. Realise the difference between a healthy ego and bragging, what is mature and what is immature. A healthy ego has already proven the point; the braggart is insecure and reminds you constantly.

4. Can state your point of view affably, not shove it down someone's throat to win at all costs. It's not a contest; it's a conversation.

5. Hold your tongue, and do not say what you want simply because you 'had to get it off your chest'. That's the 'Can we be open'? sort of question, often immaturity masquerading in an adult body.

6. Don't interrupt or finger jab aka, the 'winner-take-all' conversation.

7. Stop dismissing others who work below you with a verbal flick of the wrist of 'You don't really know', or the 'I'm smarter than you' attitude, which we have all been exposed to at one time or another.

8. Don't give people the 'You must be out of your mind/I can't believe you said that' look, usually done by those who prey on others below them.

9. Thank people, regardless of who they are or their status. We all swim in the same waters, and no one, absolutely no one, is above thanking others.

10. Know how to apologise—and damned quickly. I am not referring to cross-cultural apologies (easily and often done in certain cultures), but the apology needed to get on with the work at hand.

In the words of Rabbi A. J. Heschel, 'When I was young, I admired clever people. As I grew old, I came to admire kind people'.

The Tao of Affability

Sitting around with other parents one weekend, we discussed an article, which addressed high school behaviour, principals, students, cliques, and political correctness. Many of the parents disagreed with most of the article's content and premise. I eventually piped up and stated why I essentially agreed with the author.

I may have changed some of the parents' perspective, but when I thought about it later, I doubt I made any allies in airing my thoughts. I'd gotten irritated with some of their comments, so I aired my thoughts in an overly ham-handed, jousting way. Who wants to lock horns in what was meant to be a socially convivial setting? Clearly I needed to temper my delivery (and I daresay behaviour) in such situations.

But my pugnaciousness paled in comparison to what I encountered on another night not long after at a cocktail party, watching three women politely listen to a hedge fund manager from the United States hold forth. From what I gathered, none of the women knew much about hedge funds, but it was a social chit-chat, and small talk is the essence of such gatherings.

The hedge fund guy was apparently not only maladroit in his small talk but verbally belligerent. He browbeat, berated, interrupted, and talked down to the ladies, alluding to how ignorant they were about Wall Street, finances, taxes, and more or less everything. Indeed, one of the three women, who never says anything negative about anyone, walked away, saying how uncomfortable it was listening to him.

The point of these two situations I was involved in? Behaviour and affability.

Affability is defined as being easy going, gracious, genial, and amiable. Not quite the same thing as *being kind* (also extremely important) or *nice* (too broad) or *humorous*, or *quick-witted*, nor even all the talk of *charisma*. Rather it is the trait of someone who has a light and easy touch with others.

Why is this important? Aren't we splitting hairs? Absolutely not. Having a good nature, being pleasant and friendly around those who may not be, is imperative.

Being affable gives one latitude, and others cannot rush to judge you harshly. Affability is not grounded in lobbying to get others to approve of you; affability (as opposed to being nice) is how you feel about yourself, and thus how you act towards others.

That light touch is so, so critical because people warm to those who bring a bit of warmth. Being affable does not mean that no one knows what you think or what you stand for. Far from it. One can have pointed and strong opinions, but if the delivery is done in an affable way, that makes all the difference.

Knowing where one stands is important; whether one agrees or not is secondary. Affability is not didactic, nor ponderous, confrontational, or obtuse.

Had I modified my initial thoughts to engage a smile from the people I was with, I would have likely had future dialogue with them based on comfort. I came out swinging, made my point, but hardly affably. Had the boorish guest merely listened, smiled, and made a few small jokes, the women at that party would not have spent the weekend spewing invectives about hedge fund managers.

We all get so caught up in being right—and being the first to say how right we are—that we overlook the tremendous importance of a smile, a nod, a warm word, and some eye contact, all with a pleasant disposition. This is not a Miss Manners' column, it is Leadership 101, and if you think of leaders whom you admire, you'll see exactly what I mean.

Stop, Listen, and Wise Up

There are those who revel in being contrarians, doing the opposite of what others expect. On occasion, it can be advantageous; catching an opponent off guard and using it to bolster one's position, and knowing when to do so is a strength. But it can also be the domain of those who think they know more than they do, with a ready list of excuses when something doesn't work or get done.

I should know. As a teen and young adult, I moved against the grain of many of my teachers, not giving them what they had asked. My grades reflected it, but I had the hubris to blame it on them for overlooking my innate talent. An attitude (I'm loath to admit) that carried on longer than it should have.

At work you'll see that attitude in those who cannot stand their bosses, bad-mouthing them as dolts, whining that the company has no direction, that management won't listen to their ideas, generally displaying the 'screw 'em' school of thought.

What do such people do? Complain, dig their heels in, obfuscate, cross their arms, lecture others about their shortcomings, and pontificate how the company overlooks talent. They'll state that only sycophants and apple polishers get ahead, spending time doing everything except what they're supposed to do.

The axe falls and they are quickly beheaded. Exiting, they remind anyone still listening how much they disliked working there anyhow, how underappreciated and overlooked they were, thankfully now onward to new companies where the sun always shines. But, lo, the same thing happens again and again until they hit a wall.

The lesson is not merely to respect elders, though that's a start. People who have been around longer than you, whether teachers, bosses, peers, (and let's not forget parents) know a fair amount if you're willing to drop your dukes and listen. Caveat: Not everyone has wisdom oozing from each pore; some people are the same as they were forty years ago, stuck in a time warp. But they're not whom I'm referencing.

Cut down on the arrogance, and do what is not natural: listen more and talk less. Use the Golden Rule and walk in someone else's shoes before you comment. Realise your problems, when compared to the billions on Earth, are not insurmountable. Indulge in a dose of humility. Smile more, be nice to strangers every so often, laugh more often, and don't go around correcting others; do it to yourself first.

I think of Lee Kuan Yew as I write this, and, of course, he is an exception. His school of charm and etiquette would blow up the region, as he revels in saying exactly what he wants, damn the consequences, tossing *bon mots* out and letting them land where they will. I admire him and agree with much of what he says. When one is in one's late eighties, with a new book published, calling it as it is, and a 'founding father' of Singapore, it is tolerated, and much is to be learned from him.

But most of us are not in that position. We need to think more carefully about how we act, and how others view us. When we do write or speak, we must think of the impact on our surroundings, our audiences, our superiors, subordinates, peers, children, parents, and learn how to move with grace and facility at each turn.

It can be done. The sooner one learns it the better.

Social Media Cross-culturally: US ≠ ROW[11]

An article in the *New York Times* discussed how too much online information is shared within a business context.[12] Written by an executive coach, the author touched on the corporate challenges of too much openness and even created a handle for this dysfunction, which she calls OSD, Obsessive Sharing Disorder.

What caught my eye was a single cross-cultural comment. The author mentioned to a British colleague, she was now seeing 'that many Americans were starting to realise that they reveal way too much about themselves'.

Absolutely.

It is not technology that makes everyone talk more about themselves. Social media highlights what many Americans have always done. Unlike many Asians or Europeans, Americans are more apt to talk openly about their lives, with strangers or friends. It's a long-standing cultural tradition, I suppose, from US presidents revealing their inner selves (or external, when US President Lyndon Johnson lifted his shirt to reporters to show his surgical scars) to seatmates whose life stories surface during a plane ride, to celebrities or criminals telling all.

The 'hail fellow well met' profile is what makes Americans endearing— their generosity and gregariousness to others. It is also antithetical to non-Americans. In Asia, it is not likely for people to openly or readily share personal details. (I'm talking in relative, not absolute, terms).

I'm American, work and live in Asia, and get both sides reasonably well.

Culture still matters greatly, and such articles are often too US-centric to easily apply elsewhere. Today's companies want to think and act globally, but still lack perspective. Many management articles and coaching tips I read tilt towards a US style of communication; more direct and open— almost confrontational. This merits attention. That is to say, talking

---

[11]   Rest of the world.

[12]   Peggy Klaus, 'Thank You for Sharing. But Why at the Office'?, *The New York Times,* August 18, 2012, http://www.nytimes.com/.

cross-culturally when one thinks the way they've done it back home is the way to do it globally. Uh-uh.

I would, however, agree with the author's first bullet point, which is:

- 'Before you open your mouth about your personal life, ask yourself: Who's listening to me (a boss, a client, a colleague or a friend)'?

That is Business Politics 101 and merits reinforcing. Know your surroundings, know your audience, know how to listen more than talk, agree more than not, and take your time. Relationships anywhere in the world cannot be done without talking. That is why social media cannot foster friendships.

Acquaintanceships, yes, and good ones at that. Friendships and relationships, personal or professional, with requisite obligations, exist by talking and listening, preferably face to face. But not by sharing too much too soon, especially at work.

Mens Agitat Molem, Mind Over Matter

Years ago I worked in Los Angeles, in the airport area of Inglewood. Next door to the office was an Exxon gas station, run by an older Egyptian man. We'd often exchange a few words when I'd fill up the tank. I recall one day pulling in to the station in a foul mood, whatever had happened at the office had left me seething, and it must have shown. My friend looked at me and asked what the matter was. Brushing it aside, I said it was nothing, just the weather that was making me feel that way. He looked at me through his heavy, black-rimmed glasses, shook his head and said, 'That's the one thing you can't control' and shuffled off.

I still remember that brief exchange, long ago as it was. Of course, he was right. All your behaviour can be controlled—or modified. That much is within your control, and not at the control of elements around you.

I'm asked consistently about how the 'market' will be this year or next. I know no more than anyone else, but I try to posit a thoughtful and measured response. But that is not the important stuff.

What counts is what you have control over: how you spend your time, with whom, where, and doing what. Forget the doom and gloom about the economy, forget about the political climate, forget about the latest sabre rattling of governments. You can't control them, and such things are not important to your day-to-day existence.

What can you control? Your behaviour and attitude, your work ethic and your words, your presentation and image, your manner and deportment, your mental and physical well-being, your negativity or optimism, and your smile or frown. All are within reach. Think bountiful, not threadbare. Think opportunity, not disaster.

Think, 'The Best Is Yet to Come'.[13]

Cultural Fit

I spend a lot of time assessing whether candidates will fit within a company. The higher one goes, it is a given that you can do the job—but that is not what makes a strategic hire. Rather, the focus is on whether the person can:

- Know what to say and when to hold off
- Understand how to build internal relationships with people or teams that matter
- Perceive the dynamics and power base in an office, region, or corporation
- Have the confidence to work independently and also tap in to those when unsure
- Keep an open ear to what is being said but not necessarily be a party to the chatter
- Study the flow of power and information; know where to be and why

---

[13] The title of a classic song composed by Cy Coleman with lyrics by Carolyn Leigh, usually associated with singer Frank Sinatra.

To expound: I recently had a lunch conversation, which centred around C-level execs whom my lunch companion's company thought needed help getting to that next (and near) top-level. They were mostly Asian, had been with the company for some time, all considered valuable with high potential.

What was the help they needed? According to him, better English. *Come again?* All spoke reasonably fluent English (and I should add this company is US-based). The concern was that they were not able to speak with the fluency needed to influence top management. 'Can they learn to articulate better'? he asked.

That is the wrong question. It is *not* about English fluency; that is an archaic way of thinking about cross-cultural talent. The issue is how to have enough presence to be listened to, which requires more emotional intelligence (EQ) and influencing skills rather than fluency in English.

Here are three points to consider, applicable to both companies and employees, native English speakers or not:

1. **Know who has power, and do not shy from it.** Read the organisational chart strategically, and build alliances with people and groups that matter. Your boss may or may not be the one with clout. Build a circle which you can consistently rely on.

2. **Know how to deliver.** If you listen and watch carefully, you'll know what the boss and power bases want, what puts a smile on their faces, and has them nodding their heads. Give 'em what they want. When you don't agree, still give 'em what they want and learn how and when to politely lobby for your ideas. Arguing about what you may think is a better idea gives you more rope to hang yourself.

3. **Know how to speak with precision, measurement, and resonance.** Many people scoot or stumble through their talks, mumbling or mispronouncing, not thinking out their time in the klieg lights. Say it clearly, concisely, confidently, with some gravitas but not too much. It is *irrelevant* whether you are a native English speaker or not; *it is your presence, deportment, and delivery, not your accent.*

That is what lingers, not the tones, and sometimes not even the content. The impression remains, and that is proportional to one's presence.

Equally important is knowing when to hold one's tongue. It deserves a chapter of its own.

5

'YOU CAN'T TAKE IT BACK'

I read how one well-known CEO would critique his dinner partners at the end of the evening—from conversation content, delivery, to eye contact, providing constructive criticism. The writer, Lucy Kellaway, went on to say

> *'When he told me this I was shocked. How vulgar, I thought. Yet every time I've been out to dinner and sat next to people who were not pulling their weight, I have thought about him and wished that I was brave enough to offer tips on how they could improve'.*[14]

The moral of the article seemed to be that we should all have the nerve to do what the CEO did, as she relates her own coming-of-age, and doing so at other dinner parties.

But if it is a true story, it's wrong, wrong, wrong. All of us have been in social settings with people who did not 'pull their weight' and be able to get through a less than convivial evening with grace. Manners are the stuff that keeps much of the world together, learning how not to say what you actually think, or we'd all be in jail for some infraction.

---

[14] Lucy Kellaway, 'Why feedback forms leave me fed up', *Financial Times*, March 7, 2010, http://www.ft.com/home/asia.

Can you imagine going to a conference and raising your hand after the speaker finished to tell him or her how awful and deadening the speech was? The unspoken agreement we enter into when attending a conference is simply that people can critique it later, outside the confines of the auditorium.

You must watch carefully what you say, *especially* in a position of power or authority. One strongly worded critique from a figure of authority—professional or personal—can inflict so much damage that some people never fully recover.

Carefulness and thoughtfulness in our speech and judgments are undervalued, when in fact it should govern all our communications, whether at work, social functions, or home.

Over the weekend my daughter was out with her friends. She needed to be back at a certain time. As it got later, my ire grew. In passing, I muttered to my son that if she didn't get back soon, she'd be grounded, though I added that was unlikely, as she almost always did call. He didn't hear my last comment, and when she did call (with enough time to spare), he picked up the phone, and (as only siblings can do) was quick to tell her that she was going to be grounded.

When I got on the phone, she asked if that was true, and why. I told her that really wasn't true, and wriggled out of it, but I had ever so slightly diminished myself.

Lessons learned.

First, in life, whether at home or at work, don't let your imagination carry you away with thoughts of what someone else is (or is not) doing. Do not assume, as you'll be wrong most of the time.

More important than your thoughts are your actions and words. There is no need to share your criticisms out loud to a spouse, a child, a co-worker, or a peer. It inflicts, wounds, and what is said can't be undone. As one sage said thousands of years ago, '*Have you heard something? Keep it to yourself—you won't break'*.

Saying what you think in order to make sure everyone knows where you stand has its place and time, but at the wrong place or time, has only an adverse effect.

One final anecdote. When my teenage children were on school break, I was making lunch for my son. He finished his call on his mobile and said he'd be out in ten minutes to hang with one of his good friends after he ate. I replied with 'Seems to me your pal seems a little bossy sometimes, telling you where to go and when', erroneously linking something else I thought his friend had done.

I instantly got a laser stare and silence.

Quickly backpedalling, I said to him, 'Probably shouldn't have said that'.

He laid into me. 'You don't even know him. You don't know our conversations. You have no idea who says what. How can you possibly come to that sort of conclusion about him'?

I immediately agreed. 'You're right, I take it back. Sorry'

Then came the zinger.

He looked me square in the eye and without hesitation evenly said, 'You can't take it back'.

I actually smiled at first, thinking I've taught my kids well, always emphasizing the importance of how words can both nurture and hurt.

I told him he was 100 percent right. I couldn't take it back. I could only apologise and hope he would accept my apology. A tough lesson for a parent. He was right, and I was wrong.

The tremendous importance of watching what we say—to whom and when—cannot be overstated. Highly negative and positive words stay with us, are reread or remembered over and over again.

Negative words hurt, and those who think honesty is the best management policy are sadly mistaken. It is immaterial whether one makes a hurtful comment because it is the truth; it is almost never worth it.

Not sure of how to be candid with someone else? Wait for the right time and find the best way to phrase the correct delivery, whether email or face to face.

Have something to get off your chest? Wait a while—it won't do you any damage.

The difference between maturity and immaturity is knowing how to refrain from saying things in the heat of the moment. None of us is perfect, but we can all do a shade better with our self-control, and work on what we say, or simply hold off.

Words are like bullets; once shot they can't be retrieved. Character assassination is not an arbitrary phrase. In a day and age where we perpetually blog, email, Skype, and text, it behooves us all to slow it down a notch and sit on it for a while before we say or write it.

(My son did eventually accept my apology, by the way.)

Valid Input or Simply Argumentative?

Someone wiser than I, consultant Alan Weiss, mused in an online post about others who disagree, stating:

'Too many people respond to a new idea or suggestion with, "Let me tell you how I do it", or, "I disagree". Their immediate response is to protect their own thinking patterns or try to prove they know more [than you]'.

I replied to him, stating that I disagree regularly. It's *how* you disagree, and whether you do so with aplomb and grace. Anyhow, I continued, having a healthy dollop of scepticism may well result in disagreements, but with all the bloviating out there, shouldn't [disagreements] be expected? As long as one's moral compass is screwed on straight, accept that disagreements are part of the fabric of life, in business or personal matters.

His reply was withering (and, of course, he disagreed).

'Disagreeing—especially regularly, makes you overly emotional, and you now sound simply argumentative. . . . I don't disagree "regularly" and yet I'm a thought leader in my field. [He is, and can back it up.] The ability to feel someone else is wrong and not have to tell them is the sign of confidence and maturity. Think about it'.

I did think about it, and quickly told him he was right. And he thanked me.

We often think *our* opinion matters, *our* voice must be heard, *our* knowledge and expertise must be clearly visible at all times. But it doesn't. Verbally crossing swords—politely or adversarially—seldom burnishes a relationship.

How do others view you after a meeting? Can you truly put yourself in their shoes? When they walk away, are they prone to think:

a) 'X is smart, but, dammit, I can't get a word in as usual. He's more concerned about his verbal pyrotechnics, defending his position, and showing he knows more than I do'.
   Or,
b) 'X is smart. He is a patient listener, funny, and comfortable to be with. He knows where he's going, what he wants, won't settle for less, and makes me genuinely feel better about myself'.

Here is an excerpt of an interview I just read with well-known chef Mario Batali:

'Realise you're not the most important or the most intelligent person in the room at all times. Understanding that is a crucial component of the kind of self-deprecation that makes someone really good at understanding other people, especially when they're faced with their own limitations and they come to you for help. It's about being able to empathize and understand and communicate, even under stress, in a way that helps them solve a problem, as opposed to becoming part of the problem. *The first day a chef believes that he or she knows everything is the first day for the rest of their life that they will be a jerk, because you can't know everything'.*[15]

Takeaway point: You are never the most important person in the room at all times, and if you are trying to prove your importance, you will be— as Chef Batali stated—a jerk.

Not having to prove yourself to others, even if they're clearly off base, exudes confidence in yourself and comfort with others.

The need to always be right will remain the domain of the churl, child, or politician. Ask yourself, 'How often do I disagree'?

If you say 'regularly' as I did, some soul-searching might well be in order. Tamp down on the need to prove yourself, and you may find a liberating result.

---

[15]   Adam Bryant, 'In Mario Batali's Kitchen, You'll Refrain from Shouting', *The New York Times*, August 25, 2012, http://www.nytimes.com/.

6

WORKING WITH THE DIFFICULT BOSS

A coaching conversation over a coffee not long ago:

'I'm looking around, curious to see what else is out there'.

'Anything in particular that is spurring you on right now to look'?

'Do you know my boss'?

'Yes, but not well'.

'He and I are very different—I consider myself more diplomatic, quieter, I guess, and less confrontational. However, he's been with the company a long time, and I would say he has the corporate DNA in his system. He's also more direct, more top down, that sort of thing. Actually, he thinks he can coach his team, but he basically just tells them what to do, he can't coach'.

'And that's why you want to leave? He sounds like most of the bosses I know'.

'He doesn't respect work experience—he speaks the same way to someone with twenty years' experience as he will to a recent college grad'.

'That can work positively or negatively, no'?

'That's not what I meant—it's how he treats his team, like lackeys: "Do this, not this, do that, and do it exactly this way", and so forth, no room for other opinions'.

'Ah, okay, I hear "micromanager". But again, hardly unique. Is that reason [enough] to leave'?

'I guess you could say he's a micromanager. He doesn't exactly look over everyone's shoulder, only he wants things done his way. I've gotten so tired of it. I'm not answering him now'.

'What do you mean'?

'He sends me emails asking for this and that, all sorts of petty stuff to do'.

'And'?

'And I don't answer him'.

'And'?

'He sends more emails'.

'And'?

'And I send him back a note saying it's [not one of my work responsibilities], but if he wishes to discuss it face to face, that's fine'.

'So you're not answering your boss' emails, and you're telling *him* how to communicate to *you*? That's novel'.

'Well, I don't like the way he almost bullies me and others around'.

'Er, telling your boss how you want to be communicated with is not going to win you points'.

'I realise that, so that's why I wanted to ask you if you know what else is out there'.

'Haven't a clue. But don't you think you need to fix the internal problem first? Is your job secure'?

'I should think so; I'm excellent at what I do'.

'But I'd reckon your boss may not feel the same way you do at the rate things are going. Are you spending any time internally to talk to others and see what is being said—about you, about him'?

'Not much, and I suppose that can't hurt. But I really want to get out, that's why I wanted to talk with you'.

And that is where we left it. I don't know whether my questions helped or not, but that job won't remain long-term, regardless of how flawlessly it may be executed. The old maxim of 'You can't win a fight with your boss' was basically my rejoinder.

Difficult bosses. We've all had them. Eliminate the judgmental negativity and spend more time giving the boss what he wants, consider the advice in this chapter, and at least gain some balance before looking elsewhere.

Please, Please Me

I had coffee with a woman who is general counsel for a US-based consultancy. She reminisced about her first job twenty-some years ago, working with a senior partner in a law firm who was a notorious SOB. His reputation was to intimidate and grind down those who were supposed to help him. I'll let her continue:

> 'I would see these young associates—I was one of them—come out of his office in tears all the time, and I'd think "Am I nuts? How the hell am I going to work a bully?" But actually we ended up getting along wonderfully, one of the best bosses I ever had'.
>
> 'Great to hear. You skipped a few steps in your story. How did you do it'?
>
> 'At the start, everyone came up to me and asked how I could possibly work for him. And when I'd sit in his office, he'd turn to me and say, "I know everyone says I'm difficult, and I am. But I really don't mean to be, it's not intentional."'

'Got it, but what did you do to make peace'?

'Two things. First, I gave him more information than he needed. I figured if he was going to ride me, I'd over-load him. So if there was a brief or report or research, I'd do the work but give him more info than he could pos-sibly read. It was overkill, I suppose, but if he wanted the information, I was going to give him more than he could handle and show I was up for it. And the work was quality effort'.

'What happened'?

'Over time—actually not even that long, after a few months—he started to say, "All right, no need to give me all that. I'm too busy. You know what you're doing." And that was my "aha" moment. He'd started to trust me and trust my work. Not that he didn't challenge me, but he saw my work output, liked most of what he saw, and [knew he] didn't have to chase me. And once I had his trust, we were a team. I covered him and he covered me.

'The second thing: At the start I told him I had a short fuse. I knew he did, but so did I. I explained I angered quickly. I'm not sure how much of any effect that had, but I remember that it was not easy saying that to a new boss, but I said it evenly and professionally. I figured I needed to let him know. I was open, candid, but displayed little emo-tion in my talks with him. I had to think about it, as it did not all come naturally. . . . He trusted me, and for a young associate to be able to have worked so closely with him, I learned far more than I could have otherwise.

'So now, fast-forward a couple of decades, I have some young employees come into my office and complain that their boss doesn't understand them, doesn't acknowledge their work, ignores them, and on and on. They don't get it yet. They're unsure how to give the boss what he or she wants and enough of it until the boss knows what they're doing. Some of these new hires think it's all about them, and it never is. Don't be scared of the boss, understand how to communicate and deliver—the way the boss wants it communicated. I know it sounds like a cliché, but it is so true'.

It is, and it bears repeating: Know what the boss wants, and how to present it the way *he or she* wants it, not the way you want it. If you over-deliver no one will scream—but they certainly will if you under-deliver. Find out what the boss wants, and how he or she wants it communicated. Find out how to support them in their job, never by asking them to solve your problems, regardless of whether they tell you to come in and talk anytime. Respect the title. You don't have to like it, but you have to respect it.

The boss-subordinate relationship is not even. Never has been, never will be. The boss will gladly and consistently help, but *only* after you've proven yourself—repeatedly and reliably—not a minute before.

Rule Number One: Understand How to Communicate with Your Boss

Many people I coach have challenges communicating with their boss. They often think the boss automatically understands them, and what worked previously for them will work again with another company or boss.

One person commented that he greatly respects his boss as someone smart, experienced, knowledgeable, and learned. But he has managed to rub his boss the wrong way more than once, the most recent kerfuffle over an email (and I should add the boss is in Europe, while my friend is in Asia).

'He yelled at me after I sent an email. I couldn't believe it. Is he nuts'?

'What was the email'?

'Just an "FYI". I sent him a note on something we had done, and simply said, "FYI". And for this he gets mad'?

'Tell me more'.

'There *is* nothing more to tell, that was all I did'.

'What exactly did he say to you'?

'He said, "What do you expect me to do with it?" Well, obviously nothing, that's why I *wrote* "FYI". Am I losing my mind'?

'No, but do you see his point'?

'I don't see it at all'.

'You did not say what he should do with the email. Was he supposed to read all of it—or only part? Did he need to answer? Was it okay if he ignored it? Did you want him to distribute it to others in the company, or discuss it with you first? The guy probably gets more emails than he knows what to do with, and you gave him extra work with no guidance. Do you see [the problem] now'?

'It was an FYI, for God's sake'.

'How do you communicate best with him? Or, I should say, how does he like to communicate'?

'Phone seems to work best'.

'So, more of a listener than a reader'?

'I guess'.

'After a year [with him] you should know. Sounds to me that you're not being precise in your communication with him—or at least what you think is precise is ambiguous to him, and you know who's going to win that argument. The boss only has so much time. If you're going to email, don't burden him; guide him'.

The issue of concise communication—especially when communicating with the boss—is crucial for work success.

How does your boss like communication: phone, face, text, email, Skype? Alone, with a group, regularly, formally, informally? Is he a reader or listener, visual or not, just the bottom line or two pages, actively involved or distant, emotional or aloof, organised or scattered, intellectual or visceral, Socratic or circuitous questioning? You get the picture.

Whatever the style, don't think what may have clicked with a previous boss will click again—it is always work in progress. Modify your style accordingly and see what happens. You may never end up as best mates, but you're looking for as much parity as possible to build on.

I'm not sure my friend will change his ways yet. But he will when it's important enough to him. We'll see.

Another story along the same lines: A senior exec was telling me about a more senior exec within the organisation (senior vice president and regional managing director) and how his style was confrontational with everyone.

> 'At first I couldn't stand him—all he would do was pick, pick, pick at everyone, me included. Our turning point occurred over a policy decision I had to make. I'd gotten all the regional input I needed from everyone, made sure I had the info lined up and had a well thought-out plan to implement the decision. I laid it all out for him, and what does he do? He questioned my decision—hard—and I fought back, and we went around and around. He finally stopped, agreed with what I wanted to do, and that was that. I asked him later, one on one, whether he thought his management style was really effective.
>
> 'He looked at me and said, "Yes, I really think it is. I prod people because I know they can always do better, and I want them to do their best. And if it means that I have to push them hard to get to that level, so be it. Some will deliver, and others won't, and I get rid of the deadwood."
>
> 'Personally', my friend continued, 'I don't think that's the right way, and a lot of people will not work for him. But I understand what he's trying to do'.

You could read this and think the boss a 'lunatic', and be well within your rights to think so. The world is full of people like that, and anyone who has been in business long enough has worked with such people. How do you deal with it? Everyone is different, so I can't give a one-size-fits-all answer, but I will repeat that you have to understand how to communicate to the boss and learn to complement his or her strengths.

Each boss works differently. Some are readers, some are listeners. Some like long reports, some like graphs and PowerPoints, some like one-paragraph summaries. Some want in at the beginning of a project, others don't want to know about it until it's nearly done. Some rely on one opinion (theirs) or want to have four or five different opinions before they come to a conclusion. Some foster confrontation, others want no stress in front of them. And so on.

Rule number one: Understand how to communicate with your boss.

What does your boss do unusually well? Numbers? Sales? Public speaking? Big picture and in the details? Every one of us can say what our boss can't do. So what? It doesn't matter.

Rule number two: Understand and complement your boss' strengths, and stop lamenting over what the boss needs to improve; it's irrelevant.

Help! The Boss Just Stole My Work Again . . .

A friend (I'll call him Joe) had taken a job half a year ago at a large multinational corporation (MNC), having been asked to join the business by an old ex-colleague (let's call him Frank) who had just started there himself.

Joe took the offer, and he and Frank were now the regional support team, though with Frank in a more senior position.

He soon discovered Frank would not allow him to communicate directly with anyone in the organisation; Frank had to have everything channelled through him. The regional managing director (MD) would contact Frank and tell him to write a policy position. Frank would tell Joe he was too busy and have Joe write the paper. Joe did, Frank took the paper, cut and pasted it, and sent it back to the boss. The boss thought it was great, and Frank got all the credit.

If someone of power sauntered into Joe's office, Frank would later storm in to Joe's office, reminding him that he was the boss, protocol was that senior management would go to Frank first, not Joe.

Joe relayed a couple more stories about Frank who was always out of the office, but always calling Joe to see where he was and to remind him of what he was supposed to be doing. What Frank *did* do well was look good to his boss, and there is an art to that.

Most of us have experienced a boss who steals work, calls it their own, micromanages, trusts no one, and puts loyalty above everything else. They're always around, and running away from them solves nothing.

Such people have to be managed differently. In any mid-sized to large corporation, other people watch—they always do. When they watch, there are opportunities to raise one's own visibility, to promote one's accomplishments. It can be done without crushing the boss or braying, but nicely, ethically, and firmly, so people know what you've done, where you've contributed, and where you're going.

Previously in this chapter we discussed how to work with a difficult boss, but sometimes there's no dealing.

Case in point: Many years ago I worked with an Austrian who'd lived in Hong Kong for many years. He'd just been hired as the regional MD the same time I started with the company. His lunacy was raging paranoia, Teutonic disciplinary measures augmented with a manic-depressive personality. He ripped up the regional office staff—human carnage—a few left quickly, realising his vindictive character.

But most stayed (I was one of them) and put up with the insanity, hoping it would go away. It didn't, of course. He hired his old cronies and increased regional profit (through blood-letting), bolstered his power, and managed upward quite smoothly with the global HQ.

Whenever one of the overseas heavyweights came to town, everything was choreographed; whom they would meet internally and externally, what he wanted them to see—or not—all down to a tee. He cloistered them in day-long meetings, and I recall a couple of the senior vice presidents (SVP) demanding time to walk around and speak with the staff. They did, and Lunatic Boss shadowed them to make sure nothing untoward was said.

It was almost like being in a prison and wanting to shout, 'Don't you see how we're being treated'? but not being able to do so. I'd never experienced anything like that before. But we were all free agents and could have left at any time. Eventually, I resigned, and he made me work my three-month notice in its entirety, for no logical reason, and gave me a ton of work to do, as if it mattered.

He stayed there for a few more years, eventually imploded, and should have never had that job in the first place.

The lunatic boss will have these characteristics:

- Often be manic, likely misstate what you have said, turn it around or deny it, be adept at making you feel that any business slips or errors are all your fault, not theirs.
- Mentally browbeat the staff, making you question your self-worth and take away your ability to impact (lunatics cannot empower; they hold on to power for dear life).
- Tease or mock you if threatened by your presence, intellect, or ideas—and if it's a good idea, will often steal it.
- Never make you part of the inner sanctum if you cannot agree with their views. Loyalty counts for everything to them.
- Only share ideas or information that benefits them and are less interested about the welfare of the organisation.
- Seldom solicit your opinion, but rather try to catch you off-guard to maintain a power advantage—checking in at odd times of the day or week to see what you're doing, and pick on minutiae to show their control.

Perhaps, most important, you will never learn, nor get smarter or more confident with a lunatic boss. You will, however, spend your time anxious, afraid of making a mistake, which forces people to cower.

It's all regressive and dictatorial behaviour. If any of the above is what you're currently up against, get out and don't look back. If you've emphatically nodded your head to two or more of the above bullet points, make the move. Life is far too short to be with a boss who diminishes you.

7

THOSE CORPORATE GAMES

In this chapter I highlight some of the more consistent corporate political posturing I've witnessed.

The point is *not* to say, 'What a shame people behave so poorly', but to be cognizant of what you may be ignoring or don't know how to handle, but to think through the various personalities and behaviours at work.

NIMBY (Not In My Back Yard): The turf war executive who has a territory/region, a piece of the business, and guards over it zealously. Concerned about possessions only, he'll have the 'He who has the most toys wins' bumper sticker, gauging his effectiveness and worth by the size or revenue of the fiefdom he controls. Don't step into his yard without asking permission; you'll get shot.

I Never Said That: The exec who reverses what is said in private when in public (or vice versa), and. if asked, will often reply with a shake of the head, a smile, and say, 'I think you've got that wrong. I never would have agreed to that'. Confusing? One of the hardest things with such people is they make you unsure whether you're hallucinating or forgotten what you said the day before. Practised at the art of the subtle lie to keep you off balance, their body language and words reveal little. Even if cornered, they'll usually wriggle free, saying that was not what they meant. Few emails, and hard to nail.

Am I Paying You to Think or to Do as You're Told?: The best advice I can give young grads entering their first corporate job is: The boss is always right. 'When I need input, I'll tell you' attitude still very much exists at senior levels of management. The subordinates who don't understand how their superior thinks and behaves will often overdo it and try to outshine the boss. They will soon be drawn, quartered, and executed.

She's Great, But . . . : Almost all of us use this one, the backhanded compliment, which can make or break careers. The reason for its prevalence is that no one in an organisation likes to openly rip apart someone else, so the shredding is often couched in polite terms. When taken to new heights of negativity and criticism, however, you need to be aware. Here are some lines I've actually heard:

> 'Oh, she's terrific. The way that girl can drink, party animal! I've never seen anyone so tiny drink so much—isn't she something'?
>
> 'That project presentation you put together is very, very impressive. But have you thought about where the funding will come from? Don't you know how tight they are? There is no question they'll reject it. Did you think it through before putting so much effort into this'?
>
> 'I heard he wants to get into management and run the BU. He really is a great guy, a little rough around the edges with the staff, but he is so good in sales, it would be hard to lose that revenue if he was running a BU. I personally think in another year or two he'll be more polished, don't you'?

When you hear such things at the office, don't ignore them because you're too busy. Do you really know what is being said about you? Not what you assume is being said, but what is actually being said. Ignore the buzz at your own peril.

Selective Editing: Ubiquitous at the office, but it can be taken to dizzying heights. A major presentation is given, and the only information shown is to clearly support a certain point of view, even if there is known contrary evidence or numbers by others in the room. Withholding or shading information, the presenter is [sometimes] able to create new but misleading conclusions to get what he or she wants, whether staff, budget, promotion, or to squash the competition, internally or externally. Everyone wants to put their agenda, department, or budget in the best light, and that's expected. What I'm addressing is a more aggressive and deceptive angle.

Don't Take It Personally (or 'I'm Only Trying to Help You'.): Instead of talking about you behind your back, some people are quite adept at the art of the backhanded compliment to your face (almost always in front of others for greater impact), and you get unexpectedly dinged. If left unchecked, it'll happen repeatedly because you're easy prey. Such people need to be called on it and confronted. And when they respond with 'Aw, c'mon, don't take it personally', don't let up. It's all personal, isn't it? We don't yet work with robots. An organisation is people, tethered together through contracts and similar goals. Don't let such cavalier stuff go. Address it and bury it—nicely, politely, and firmly.

The Blame Game: Usually done by mid-level or senior management who direct their insecurities or inabilities towards their boss or company. For example, 'I'd be so much further along in my career if _____ was a better/more dynamic/insightful/friendly/smarter/helpful boss who could get things done'. When directed towards the company, the patter seldom changes: how 'they' can't get it right, 'they' are not well run, all corporate initiatives are bound to fail, 'I should be at _____, where they really value talent'.

If You Say So: Almost always done by existing staff to new management. A new leader arrives, often both interest and resentment co-mingle. When the new boss decides on directions or strategy, some of the naysayers—many long-time employees—will go along but quietly try to drag it down. They'll mutter that it's been tried before, so when the strategy doesn't quite succeed as planned, there will be comments of 'I told you it wouldn't work'. The new boss must first determine who is with him, who is indifferent, and who is unhappy with the changes. Again, ignore at your own peril.

Gotcha: Done when a senior exec wants to nail someone else, but can't easily fire them. If he or she has the power, they'll change the rules of the game: new and early mornings to report in; late night or unannounced meetings or calls; requesting reports with unreasonable time frames; and piling up work demands, which won't be used or applied. Most of this is done to have the employee throw his or her hands up and quit. Sometimes it works, sometimes not. There are many variations on a theme with this one.

Hold That Temper: This is when an exec has a well-known, hair-trigger temper, and when crossed, a tantrum is thrown. The big scenes are regularly played out, often with some visibility. It is simply easier not to cross such people; they often get what they want, or are left alone. Akin to a child screaming, usually placated until they stop. Most execs with short fuses don't last too long if they want to climb the corporate ladder, but can wreak havoc along the way

Comeback Kid: When you verbally corner another person, suddenly the tables are turned and you're accused of some sort of error. Another easy way to spot this type: nothing is ever their fault. Ever.

Managing Upward: Remember, I'm giving examples *in extremis*, as we all must learn how to manage upward. These are people who focus only on their bosses, or board, or stakeholders, usually extremely polished. Not quite sycophancy, but not far behind. Their audience-the senior stakeholders-seldom view it the same way you do, and are likely to hold such people in high esteem most of the time.

A recently promoted friend had to compete for a new role with another person whom I will call Ace. Ace was quite astute at managing upward, always made sure he delivered on what was asked (though seldom acknowledged the work of his staff to senior management) and was regarded well within the company. My friend had Ace's number. The boss, however, didn't see it. He was far too busy and not overly concerned, as long as the results were on target.

When the new position opened up, she and Ace applied. She had better deportment and presence, along with a more supportive network. The promotion went to her, and Ace became her subordinate with a direct line into her.

I asked how Ace was taking the new reporting structure.

"Great', she said. 'He has had a complete turn-around, he's helpful, he's cooperative, I've had a number of talks with him, and he is onboard with me and the team.

But, of course, I don't trust him one bit.

I figure he'll go back to his old ways at some point. So while it's great that he's changed and become a team player, I keep my foot on him, lightly but firmly nonetheless. I know he's waiting for an opportunity to pounce. But that's okay, I'm ready'.

She's likely right, and savvy enough not to get fooled by the wolf in sheep's clothing. The same applies for you. The Reaganism of 'trust but verify' is a sane way to work within a matrix organisation. If you work with an Ace-type coworker, pay attention, and do *not* get caught off guard.

My Way or the Highway: These execs order and intimidate. Filial piety and absolute loyalty is demanded from those below them, hence utter control. Challengers will be gone quickly, not a collaborative environment, as most everyone is on their own and prove their individual worth. In order to maintain such control, the boss must always know what everyone's working on in order to keep the reins tight. They also are likely to complicate the simple. Anything which can be done in three steps takes nine. This is not due to disorganisation, but extreme micromanagement and perfectionism.

It's easy to deduce that if one always triple checks, exploits information about others, takes extra time to complete a project, covers up with élan, uses haste and pressure rather than a steady pace, and never takes ownership of errors (only successes) then you should either pack up and move on, or have the top management weed them out.

This list might seem too cynical. But the intent is to highlight patterns we all observe—or do ourselves. The more one recognises a few of these patterns, the more likely one can both predict the outcome and change what you have control over.

Need practical advice when facing people of the above calibre? Read on.

Watch Your Back

A former senior hedge fund manager, who now works on his own, paid his dues throughout many years in the i-banks. For quite some time he ran the Asia-Pac investment-banking practice for white-shoe financial institutions. When we caught up for coffee, he told me the following story:

> 'There was this young guy who worked for me, very bright, very ambitious A-type, as all i-bankers are, and managing them was never easy. This guy, however, had real star potential. He also had a very tight relationship with my boss, whom he knew before he took the job with my team. I knew they were close, but was never bothered by it.
>
> 'He was doing a pretty good job, and I had no large issues with him—until I found out one day that he was in one of our other regional offices, walking around with a clipboard and advising everyone of a restructure—and at the top of the list was that I was being made redundant!
>
> 'After I found out, I called my boss and said: "I'm firing him within twenty-four hours. The only way I won't fire him is if you fire me first." And boy, was my boss furious'.
>
> 'Furious with this guy'? I asked.
>
> 'No, actually. He was furious with *me*. He yelled at me over the phone, warned it would be a big mistake, made all sorts of excuses on his behalf, that he didn't mean it, reminded me how valuable his was to the team, to the bank, he just needed more time to grow, and so on. Not a happy

boss, for sure. But to his credit, he didn't stand in my way. And the guy was gone within a day. When you have to fire someone in those circumstances, the chances are, in their heart of hearts, they know what's coming anyhow'.

Jack Welch was famous for saying, 'If you see a snake in the grass, kill it'. One does not stand there waiting to be bitten. You go after the threat and deal with it as it is, not trying to wish it away.

Often the threat is manageable. People may be scared of revealing the snake for what it is, venomous and dangerous. But such situations are frequently solved by groups courageous enough to surround the snake; one person is seldom equipped for such fights. In the workplace, some are paralyzed by fear, worried of the consequences from a strong or quick action against another. When there is a snake lurking close by, whether a boss, peer, or subordinate, never be scared to act, especially if there has been an ethical breach.

My friend concluded, 'The very worst my boss could have done was fire me. And if he had, so be it. Wouldn't have killed me'. The snake, however, would have died inevitably.

In contrast, here's an example of a situation in the making: Another friend, a regional director, had recently hired someone (working elsewhere in the region). The new chap was doing well; smart guy, good pedigree and contacts, presented well and 'made a contribution from day one'.

My friend mentioned that his boss had been with the global CEO the previous week, advising the CEO on a new trade association presidency he'd been asked to serve, a prestigious association with many senior government officials. This new hire had flown overseas to help as it involved a geographic area the new hire knew quite well.

My friend was off-site and couldn't make that meeting, but didn't think much about it. He knew his subordinate had more market knowledge than he did and encouraged him to attend.

I asked how they all got along, my friend's boss, my friend's subordinate, and the global CEO.

'Very well', he replied. 'This guy knows his stuff, and it was a big plus for our team'.

'Who briefed you'?

'I heard from my boss, who was happy with the way it all turned out with the CEO'.

'Did you speak to your subordinate'?

'Actually, I didn't. He sent a recap of everything to my boss, but not to me'.

'Really? Why not'?

'Don't know, but I told him to please send me a copy, which he did'.

'How long has he been onboard'?

'Three months'.

'He should have copied you. Don't you think that's a bit bold'?

'I did, but told him to please CC me in the future'.

'It wouldn't hurt to remind him of the pecking order, which he should know well enough'.

My hunch is this subordinate (if he is as ambitious as my friend says) will do it again. He's already had a taste, and it can intoxicate.

My friend shrugged it off, busy with other tasks. If he does not watch it, this guy will run around him and try to take his job: the warning signs are there. Managing the overly ambitious requires astuteness of leadership, intuition, and keeping one's ear to the ground, the same way it would be with a boss who tries to push you aside—they are in all shapes, sizes, and levels.

Your career is not decided only by superiors, as those below or to the side can be equally helpful or deleterious.

To close this chapter, I relate a sad story of a situation caught too late: A senior professional with nearly thirty years' work experience, in his current role for nearly four years, asked to meet me. He was looking to make a move soon, ideally to a similar sort of role.

'What's your timeline', I asked.

'Not sure', he said, 'as I'm still working, but not sure for how much longer'.

'Budget cuts, re-org'? I asked.

'No', he said, in his very matter-of-fact, low-keyed tone, 'the woman I hired earlier in the year to work under me has just taken my job, and I now report to her. She told me the other day that she thought I would sabotage the projects we're working on, and told me to just take a payout and go, although I'm not sure when that is'. He gave me a weak smile.

'Hang on. The woman that *you* hired, who reported to *you*, is now your boss? Did you see it coming'?

'No, had no idea until my boss, my old boss, that is, called to tell me that I had a new boss'. Another weak smile.

'How did that happen? There must have been some warning signs, no? Were you considered a marginal employee'?

'No, far from it. I've only received very, very good appraisals, so nothing like that'.

'Who can you speak to, who's in your corner? Who are your true supporters, your allies within the organisation'?

'Well, the person who was my biggest supporter left last year, and there really isn't anyone since then who is really in my corner, a couple sort of, but not many'.

'What are you going to do'?

'Probably just go and get away from this place. It's obviously not a good environment. I suppose I should have seen it coming, as I was warned by one of our old ex colleagues about her. I guess I should have paid more attention to that. Oh, well'. Another polite smile. 'My wife said it'd be best not to rock the boat, to just move on and forget about it'.

'And what do you think you should do? Walk away and take what is offered? Keep at the job and tough it out? Fight it'?

'I think I should fight it', he said, and that was the first time I thought maybe he actually had the fight in him to do it.

'Good', I said, 'and line up your alliances. Don't let her bully you. Two can play this game. If you do exit, make them pay for it, as this is a completely unfair dismissal'.

This stuff frequently happens in business, and in this case, he was a flyweight fighting a heavyweight. He didn't see it coming, likely focused on his work more than what was happening around him.

Don't let this happen to you. Be aware of the corporate games others around you are playing. Spend time building your alliances, especially at a senior level, and less time being a worker bee—or you get stung. More on this in the next chapter.

PART 3: STAYING ONE STEP AHEAD

8

TO THINE OWN SELF, PROMOTE

I was on the sidelines of the soccer pitch, speaking to a soccer dad I had not seen in a while:

'How's business'?

'Not bad, travelling a lot. Company's going through some restructuring. Looks like the boss here is now reporting to Sydney, instead of the United States, not sure how that will work. I'm Australian, but not sure I like this one'.

'How does it affect your job'?

'Not much, not that I can think of, but who knows'.

'How about your boss'?

'They're putting pressure on him, but not my problem. I do sales [regional sales director] and keep out of it, but he sure is getting squeezed, I can see that much'.

'If he got pushed out, who would take over'?

'Not sure, could be me, to be honest. But I don't get involved, can't stand the politics, so keep out of it'.

'But if you are a likely candidate to take over, shouldn't you at least be thinking about it, getting your profile a bit higher, not just focusing on sales'?

'Yeah, I guess so, but I haven't. Been so damned busy working and travelling. I've got to go back to the United States for a trade show next week, all the bigwigs will be there. Funny, we are having a dinner and they told me to sit at the head table'.

'Done that before'?

'Sure, a dinner every year, but no, they never asked me to sit at the head table before. Think they're trying to tell me something? [Laughs]'

'Good God, don't *you* think that means something'?

'Nah, who cares, same small talk every year'.

'Are you serious? Do you think it's arbitrary that they're putting you at the head table'?

'Haven't thought about it'.

'Don't you think you should? In case someone is feeling out your potential and asks what's going on in Asia, what you're doing, what's the growth outlook, and so on'?

'You think they'd do that'?

'*Hello*! Are you serious'?

'Well, maybe I should think about it, but not sure what I'd tell them. I hate to make it seem like I'm kissing up to them. Anyhow, we go back to Oz over Xmas and stay along the beach at my brother's place. I need a break'.

'Where in Australia'?

'Near Sydney'.

'Where is the Oz office'?

'Sydney—ah, I know what you're up to'.

'Don't you think you should pop your head in while you're there'?

'Never thought about it—nah, the boss doesn't like that. Makes me look like a apple polisher, and he keeps things close to the chest—wouldn't work'.

'Will the Oz people be in the United States at the dinner'?

'Yeah'.

'And if you told them you were in Sydney, would they not want you to come by'?

'Probably'.

'And you could tell the boss they asked you, no'?

'Ah, I get it'.

'And don't you think you need to figure out what you'll say at the dinner'?

'You're probably right. What should I say . . . '?

Soccer Dad is in his late forties, been with the company for ten years or so, done quite well, and has absolutely no sense of organisational savvy. None. But he does a good job of what he is supposed to do, and lets someone else do the rest.

By the time we parted, he was (I think) pondering my advice and figuring out what he needed to do. I have conversations like this regularly with people who are high achievers, do well at their job, but don't care to poke their head up to see what is going on around them.

The lesson here is quite simple: Do not focus only on your job. Focus on those undulating waves of influence all around you at work. Understand the importance of building your alliances with your boss and others, and be cognizant of power shifts, as they will often impact you.

Do not think that hard work alone will allow you corporate success. Hard work is a big, but insufficient, component. People who spend their time working, and working hard, often make an assumption that their boss *knows* how hard they work. It is not necessarily true, and speaks of juvenescence for those who have not learned how to promote themselves.

A senior executive lamented to me how tired he was. He never saw his family, was always working late. Tough deadlines to be met and an overly demanding boss didn't help. 'What can I do'? He shrugged.

The truth is, those who stay late are usually the drones, not bosses. Don't believe me? Look around the office. You will see those people always labouring at their desks, working and reworking their presentations, spreadsheets, emails, and reports. They often assume that if they do their *job* well, they'll get noticed or promoted. Their boss is busy doing other things, and not likely he or she knows about how late someone stays at work; the boss has enough to juggle and is seldom concerned about hours worked unless it becomes an issue.

You are not likely to impress your boss by being the last one to turn off the lights at the office, or the first to turn them on in the morning. You have a job to do, and to deliver above what is expected, in a manner that the boss wants it done. That is the primary goal. Letting the boss know what you have done, nicely, professionally, and collaboratively, is perfectly okay. If you don't toot your horn, no one hears the music. Busting your ass is not enough.

I met with a senior finance person, and we talked about one of his dotted-line reports to global HQ. 'How does he think you're doing'? I asked.

'I'm sure he knows I'm doing well', he replied.

'How do you know? Do you speak with him often, and when you do, do you tell him exactly what you have accomplished'?

'No, but I'm sure he knows. I know him quite well and have worked with him for years'.

Maybe, maybe not, and an innocuous statement, but within large global companies you have to keep your finger on the pulse, and your face in front of others all the time. Never assume your boss or anyone else in power (and power, by the way, could be anyone in the company) knows what you're working on. You gotta let 'em know. It makes a difference. Particularly if you're working overseas, far from corporate, one of the challenges is that you become remote, literally. If you have no profile back at HQ, you're in jeopardy.

Over lunch with a senior-level executive who has been with a US MNC for a few years, working Southeast Asia, he mentioned that in a year or two he'd like to consider going back to the United States on the coattails of the company. The kids may be better off, quality of life, and so forth.

'Sounds good', I said. 'How's your network at headquarters'?

'Oh, I've never been to corporate. No one has ever invited me. Not yet, anyhow'.

"Huh?" I thought to myself, but didn't say anything other than a polite 'Well, you better start your visibility plan today'. If you've never been there, how does anyone know your value there, and who are the ones who must know'? He agreed, and I suggested he start acting on it now, make a plane to get on a plane and fly back twice before the end of the year. But I shouldn't be telling a senior exec such basics.

The end of that story was that he did move back to the United States two years later. Nut not quite as planned, He was laid off from his company while still in Asia, and had to scramble to find a manager level role with a smaller company back in the Midwest, where he and his family now reside.

Here are two more examples:

The first is a friend of mine who now has a pretty good life. No longer in the corporate world (a CEO in his last role), he has a retainer from his previous company for a couple of years, steady income from rental property, and now works on deals to make equity shares, picking and choosing what he wants. *And* he knows how to promote himself—has for years. He is adept at getting on the lecture circuit, speaks at conferences regionally, then globally, and now hobnobs with the power brokers he needs to know. He gets it. On his website is a picture of him with Bill Gates to Li Ka Shing, lists of major events attended, and speeches given. It reads like someone who has a network, and that is exactly what he wants people to know.

The second example is another friend who has not figured out how to promote herself. In a new sales job for four months, she called me last month to say she did not think she would make it past the probationary period and would find out when she spoke to the boss. I asked what she thought people said about her in the office. She paused and then said, 'I think they'll say they don't know what I do'. 'Better start to promote yourself', I warned, 'and start spending more one-on-one time with those in positions of power'. Sure enough, when she had the meeting the following week, her boss told her that he would extend her probation by one month, but that she was the biggest overhead he had (as a westerner), so she'd better bring in more business soon. Last I heard, she'd had it with the company, is not interested in making any further effort, and has gotten outmanoeuvred by another peer who has been there the same amount of time, but spends all his time with the boss.

Moral of these examples? Build your brand, every day. Build it publicly, and within the organisation. Talk about what you've done, what you're going to do, in a way that does not rankle, but with a light and steady touch. Spend time with those who can keep you in your job—know their strengths and how to play to those particular strengths. Do *not* let someone else take credit for your work.

Network: Your Safety Net

What is your network? How large is it? How varied, how supportive for you is your network? If you think this is a simple exercise or question, you probably don't have the right network yet.

A case study: As I was out for my constitutional with the dog one morning, I ran into one of my neighbours. We exchanged pleasantries. I knew he'd been looking around the market and asked if he'd landed any bites.

> 'No, and actually things are getting a bit heated up there'.
> 'What's going on'?
> 'I had a meeting the other day with the new big boss and the head of HR, and was told I had three things to improve on'.
> 'Which were'?

'I had to communicate better directly to the boss, which I was told I wasn't doing. Also told I had to anticipate better, be more proactive, and that my overall work quality had to be raised'.

'Anything positive? Sounds like they tore into you . . .'

'Considering my performance review was above average and I had gotten a decent bonus last year, it's a bit confusing. It's getting a bit political there'.

(I should add that my friend is very good at the art of understatement.)

'So what are you going to do'?

'I'm thinking about my options. Obviously I'd love to get out'.

'Agreed, but in the interim, who can give you some cover, who's going to sing your praises, and diplomatically come to your defence'? I figured that was a logical question. He looked at me, pondered it, and shook his head.

'I'm not sure'.

'You've been there long enough, you've clearly gotten good reviews, there must be some people willing to go to bat for you and at least buy you some time and capital'.

Again he couldn't really think of anyone who had enough clout or presence to do so.

'I think they just want me out', he said. 'I suppose they prefer someone who is not a foreigner, and I'm an easy target if they need to cut their costs and localise'.

I wished him well and told him to let me know if there was anything I could do, and we went our separate ways.

He might have a point about localising, but a slender one at best. The bigger issue is indeed company politics, and that he has not built up his alliances at the firm. From the outside I can't say with too much clarity, but my guess is that if he is a target, it's because he has spent more of his time working than building his relationships. When the corporate turret guns are aimed, their aim is proportional to who has cover and who is a target. We've all been there.

It amazes me how many senior execs are less willing to spend the time in order to build, cultivate, and maintain their professional network. In my experience, an executive worth his or her salt will, from day one, regularly spend face time with people, over a coffee, lunch, afternoon tea, or drink.

'What'? in the day of Skype and mobile apps, you ask, 'Who has time for that'? If you could check the calendar of many senior professionals, you'd see that they are not spending their lunches at their desks, but are booked with working lunches more often than not, same for breakfasts. It doesn't mean they are working the crowd every single lunch, but they *are* spending their time interfacing with others, whether colleagues, customers, peers, or whomever. They're visible. I see them around town at breakfasts, coffees, clubs, at meetings or conferences, articles on-line, and so on, but they are not beholden to email or text. They want to see and be seen, hear and be heard. And they're in public demand more often than not.

A network is a garden. You have to water it, pull out the weeds that choke the rest, make sure there's sunlight, and tend to it, or it withers away.

A good professional network includes many different levels of support, from superiors, subordinates, peers, customers, and friends. It is not a monolithic group.

A good network lets others know what you're doing, represents and defends you appropriately, supports you in the marketplace and/or inside the company, and keeps you updated about your personal brand and reputation.

The underlying premise of your own network is to increase and maintain your physical and virtual presence. You never know when you'll need to leverage your network, and working on it when you're in a bind is too late. People, not an app, are your network. If your network is in place, this is likely a boring or irrelevant read. If, however, you don't have it at the level you should, get moving before it's too late.

Here are the lessons to learn:

Work hard, work smart, and in the process, build your name and reputation within the firm and also outside of it.

Let people know what you're working on, what you and your team are achieving. Read the organisation well enough to know who has influence (besides your boss), whom you should know, and whom to steer clear of. Familiarize yourself with the pecking order.

Know how to communicate the way the company (and the boss) communicates, and learn the art of politely talking about yourself without being a gas-bag.

Don't spend all your time 'working'.

Macho Business Culture: A Story of Power, Loss, and Travel

My lunch partner one week was from Asia with twenty plus years in the region, most of his time spent in Japan. The past five years he'd been with an overseas-based company, managing a Japan operation. He lived in Singapore for family considerations and was not interested in moving back to Japan.

> 'I wanted to meet with you to see what opportunities there may be in Singapore for me to work with a company that needs a Japan expert. I've done mergers and acquisitions, run big teams, small teams, different industries. I can handle it all'.
>
> 'I'm sure there are some. How much travel do you do'?
>
> 'At least forty, maybe forty-five, weeks out of the year, almost weekly. I'm here this week only because it's Golden Week in Japan. When I started with them the deal was that I'd commute between Singapore and Japan'.
>
> 'Almost weekly'?
>
> 'Yes, and I just signed another three-year contract with them last month. Nice group of people, pay isn't bad, I like them. They've treated me okay'.

'And the travel'?

'Well, my wife now wants me home more. Our older son is in university, we have a teenage daughter who is having some problems at home, and a younger one, so I really do need to be [in Singapore] more'.

'What are you doing about it'?

'I asked my boss, who's the CEO. He understood, said if I needed to stay a couple extra days to work things out, to go ahead'.

'A couple extra days? That's it? What's this guy like'?

'Ah, well, he travels seven days a week. He's got the global job, I'm just regional. He's always travelling, always. So what am I supposed to do'?

'And let me guess. Calls on weekends? Nighttime'?

'Oh sure, all the time. He has no concept of not working or boundaries'.

'How would you be if you could reduce your travel by half, let's just say to twice a month'?

'Twice a month? I'd be a new person, hands down, that would be a different story. But I can't. I tried to negotiate with them, but no luck. I'm the highest paid person overseas, and because I'm in Singapore and travelling, we have no office here, so I work out of the house. If I didn't travel, they'd start talking at HQ and say I'm not really working. I'd lose my job. I know it'.

'Does the CEO like you? Does he know what you contribute'?

'Oh sure he does, but I'd say 40 percent of my travel is set by HQ. They tell me where I'm supposed to be and when. I can't change that'.

'And how much money would you save the company if you reduced your travel'?

'Hundreds of thousands, I'd guess. But I can't reduce the travel. I tried to negotiate, and believe me, I did try, but couldn't do anything. I figured headhunters would be the best bet to look around for something new. And I know that's what you do. Am I wrong'?

'Yes, to a large degree you are wrong. I don't have anything to pull out of a hat. You've been in Asia more than twenty years, and you have a network that's bigger than you think, without question. You need to start thinking about it. Use your friends, your acquaintances, or strangers, and get out of this before you have a breakdown'.

'I can't quit, I have a family to support. And I'm not going to have a breakdown'.

'Sorry, I take that back. I am certainly not telling you to quit, but if you continue like this, and your daughter continues to act out or whatever it is, and it gets worse, you *will* quit. Start working your network now'.

'So, you don't know of any companies'?

'No! But you need a strategy to cope between work and travel. Do you see this? Am I making sense'?

'Yes, I hear you, and I get it. I just figured you could help me find a job'.

'I can help you think it through, sure. But I can't help give you a job, not one that you described. Not immediately, anyhow. But there are things you can start on to get there'.

Such conversations are not highly unusual: mid-life, trying to break out of a work situation and so focused on keeping the paycheque coming that he has spent no time on himself, his health, his family, and his network. And it all comes together to create the perfect storm.

In that storm is a corporate culture of machismo. He'd be trash-talked if he worked from home and was not travelling. Some companies are like that, but he has been there five years and proven himself. He'll likely survive; he's smart, canny, and it may not break him. But he's close to the precipice.

Here is my further advice to him, and to you:

Tap into your network, again and again. Rebuild your profile and take a small step back from the day-to-day job. Worker bees are at the top, regardless of the title given. Talk more about yourself, your strengths, and learn how to boast often, nicely and confidently, *not* arrogantly. We don't have to be the life of the party each time, but learn how to minimize your less loveable qualities when you want to be remembered.

Don't talk of past conquests. Be in the moment, and look forward. Some people I know still talk about their glory days from years ago, unable to move forward because they are not in the spirit of the times. Be present, not past. Know what you do well, and learn how to say it with brevity, honesty, and sincerity. It's nice to hear what others say to you about you, but the truth is you know best; hold the mirror up to your face regularly.

Do not be a victim. As Jeffrey Pfeffer so accurately writes in his book, *Power: Why Some People Have It—And Others Don't*,

> *'People sometimes give away their power by defining situations as outside their control, thereby playing the victim role giv[ing] away their power by not trying. Sometimes people don't want to "play the game", or think they won't be good at it, or can't see themselves following the strategies of successful, more political individuals. . . . we are . . . our own biggest barriers . . . because we don't make sufficient effort to build ourselves up. As Eleanor Roosevelt said, "No one can make you feel inferior without your consent"'.* [16]

I cannot emphasize this last point enough. If you think and act small, you'll be small.

---

[16] Jeffrey Pfeffer, *Power: Why Some People Have It—And Others Don't*, (New York: HarperCollins Publishers, 2010).

9

AIN'T NO ONE GONNA SAVE YOU BUT YOU

When I speak to people about what they're thinking of doing next, some appear to be steadily progressing, others are in the midst of curves being thrown at them. We all grapple with future career plans and how to transition to the next step.

Should I:

- Stay and tough it out, or just get the hell out right now?
- Take the promotion, and am I ready to do it?
- Take the payout and leave, or hang in there to see what the new management is like?
- Consider that new job offer with our competitor?
- Start my own consultancy, and be done with corporate life?
- Change careers, and do what I *really* want to do?
- Take off a few months, and regroup from the burnout?

'Would someone please tell me what the hell I'm supposed to do next'? underlies all the aforementioned questions, perfectly understandable.

I can't answer those questions, but I *can* tell you to always be thinking about how to reinvent yourself, especially if you've been in the game for a fair stretch. (By 'reinvent', I do not mean changing who you are, but rather truly taking stock of your skills and considering where else you could apply them).

In doing so, you may well answer the questions above: stay put, move across the street, change industries, hang your own shingle, do some teaching, mentor others, take a board/non-profit organization (NPO) role, or a variety thereof.

That is reinvention, it is also transition, and good for you too. Few things are more liberating and fun to do. Scary also, but the fulfilling things in life are often the least certain, and all clichés of trying and failing are applicable in this instance.

Move it up, try not to procrastinate. We get ourselves busy on minutiae and overlook taking care of ourselves, mentally and physically. If you're going to consider your transition to the next stage, no one else will do it for you. You cannot outsource your career, your life, or your health. It's yours to grow, and yours to ignore.

I frequently see those who are nearly cornered. They recognised what HQ was doing, had actually heard of significant changes that would impact them, and were told by others to prepare to move on. They nodded their heads, decided it wasn't really all that bad, worked harder to make it go away. But that's not the world we occupy.

Getting caught unaware is a lesson we all go through, but once is more than enough. Learn from it, and keep ahead of the curve. Don't get checkmated, meet the threat.

When thinking about the next act of your career, do *not* close your eyes, or wait until tomorrow, when you're in the right frame of mind, after you get hold of that one special contact, finish that one last project, or plan that business trip, which requires so much preparation. All are excuses.

I once met with someone who wanted career help. When we sat down to talk, she came unglued. Her company was going through a large re-org (whose isn't?), the team's budget had been cut, uncertainty reigned over who or what would arise from the ashes of the re-org, and she was being pulled a hundred different directions. When she regained her composure, she continued to say her two bosses had not been as supportive as she'd hoped.

'Both my bosses have disappointed me tremendously. Neither stepped up when they should have'.

I told her I've yet to come across a boss who has not disappointed me at some juncture, and so what else was new.

She did say they had recommended she get coaching. I asked her whether she found any coaches she liked.

'I spoke to a few HR had recommended. A couple I thought were okay'.

'And'?

'My bosses ultimately told me they had no budget for it, so nothing came of it'.

It was not hard to see what she needed to do, at least as a first step. I told her what I thought. She immediately replied that was *exactly* the behaviour her bosses wanted the coaching to address. Which was . . . *ta-dum*, to learn how to politely but firmly push back.

She was looking for someone, her boss, her bosses' boss, her ex-boss, her husband, her family, anyone, to help fight her battles and pull her out of the sinkhole. That is not how the world works. Expecting someone else to run interference won't last in the long run. While it's good and necessary to enlist help within an organisation to consistently steer and leverage goals, she'll need to learn how to take care of the issues herself, and be comfortable when firmly, but politely, putting her foot down when necessary.

The fact that there was no budget for coaching is not unusual. But if its importance is guaranteed, either to the coachee or management, they'll find the budget or come up with a collaborative solution. Her lack of getting coaching was symptomatic of being the victim, not knowing how to say 'no' and waiting for a rescue from others.

If and when she moves on, she will face the same situation again until she learns how to better fend for herself. The world is not a cruel place, nor an unfair one. More often than not you, and no one else, makes of it what you want. Italian tenor Andrea Bocelli said, *'Destiny has a lot to do with it, but so do you. You have to persevere, you have to insist'*.

Another story about taking control of your career: An old friend was looking for new horizons for the first time in twenty years. Smart as he was, and as well-known as he was in the market, he allowed his next career move be handled by headhunters! Because he was a known quantity, headhunters would call him, and due to a big reorganisation in his present company, he now decided to interview. Fine and well, and as a matter of fact, he was close to getting offers. Not bad, you say?

I told him to take control of his future, tap into his vast network, and get in front of the decision makers of companies he is truly interested in, which he can do in a flash. He had to relearn how to tell others about *himself*, not his company, and take steps towards increasing his visibility to the C-level people he needed to reconnect with.

Why do people outsource their career to others? Have sensible choices before you decide on your next full-time job, for goodness' sake. Look for an opportunity that appeals to *you*, not what others have said you should do.

And whatever you do, don't be a martyr. That's another hurtful attitude to one's career. These types are often too busy with their jobs, trading off personal time and reputation for the good of the company with not much left for themselves and scant time to build their professional profiles. Many are genuinely sincere and helpful, seldom turning down requests from others for help. They'll often go the extra mile if asked by a colleague (certainly a boss). They are reliable, conscientious, there when needed, and proud of being able to deliver when asked.

What the hell is wrong with that, you ask? Isn't that what we should all be doing at work anyhow? You'd be right most, but not all, of the time.

Here are some awareness points and how to stay free of this pitfall:

- The martyr usually wants sympathy—over how hard they work and struggle. Suffering can perversely make them feel superior to others because of the burdens they must shoulder.
- Recognise when the martyrdom of work has gotten the better of you. If you can't see it, or deny it, ask someone else to verify it.

- Take care of your own well-being, or you *can't* help anyone else. You'll be remembered as a martyr who nobly suffered. That is not the point of work or life. The general order is health, family, work, community, and spirituality.
- Never get so deep in the work and the company that it becomes you. It reminds me of the old temperance saying, 'First the man drinks the drink, then the drink drinks the drink, then the drink drinks the man'. Then your identity is the company's.
- Stop blaming and complaining. That's an avoidance tactic, which prevents you from dealing with life as it is. Making excuses keeps you static, not active.
- Be ready, and comfortable to anger or disappoint some people at certain times. You cannot please or make everyone happy all the time, so don't bother trying.
- Scared of saying 'no'? Practice it, by yourself, with others, and start wearing a slightly different mantle; it'll be seen and heard soon enough. And repeat the last line of the above point.

No one, I repeat, no one, wants to be remembered as a long-suffering soul who helped everyone except themselves. That is not legacy.

Take a small step if that's all you can do, but a step nonetheless. Your strengths are grounded exclusively in your actions, not through pontificating. Determine what attitude is holding you back, and push through it.

To Resign or Not: Two Tales of Unhinged Leadership

Resigning from a job is not easy. It is an admission that things did not work out. And not everyone has the 'easy' choice of resigning; some must stay put for a variety of reasons. Let me give you two scenarios of two friends, one who resigned after a year, the other who seriously considered it after two months. The common denominator: power-hungry and paranoid bosses.

Story no. 1: My friend, C-level exec, who has worked in Asia for many years, took a new job last year, after being headhunted away from a senior position to work for a smaller growing organisation. His new boss had worked his way up the ladder to become Asia-Pacific president, overseeing a large part of a publicly traded US MNC.

My friend is a stand-up guy, and I knew he was having challenges with the job. When we met, he casually mentioned he'd resigned. Why? My friend shook his head and said, 'My boss . . . It was bad. I would not tell anyone to work there, and many of us are leaving'.

At management meetings, the boss would always reply to presentations with 'Are you sure that's correct'?, focusing on one item and ripping it apart. An insecure leader, he valued loyalty first, not strengths. Those he relied on were never new hires (like my friend) but rather loyal ones. His management team was always scrounging for rumours, a control-and-command operation that had people nervous. The boss was single, his hobbies were fast cars and video games. He'd come up through the ranks, his management style unpolished, accessorized by innuendo and insecurity, which trickled down to anxiety at all levels.

My friend had worked at senior roles in a number of MNCs and never encountered this sort of behaviour before. He grappled with it for a while and tried to make a bad situation better. He enlisted a coach (company-paid) but didn't think the coach, (also beholden to the boss), quite understood the apparent viciousness.

He decided it was untenable and best to resign rather than tough it out. In his resignation, he met with the global CEO and stated why he and others were leaving. The global CEO said he knew it was a problem, but that he had other problems to contend with, Asia would have to wait, and wished him well. (Coda. My friend took a CEO role and is doing much, much better than he had been, growing from strength to strength.)

Story no.2: Another friend, a long time Asia hand, took a more senior job with a competitor. He soon realised after he started that the Asia-Pacific president viewed him as a threat and was bad-mouthing him to global HQ and other country heads. My friend is a loyal employee, had been with his previous company many years, and was not used to being shot at. He easily saw his boss' insecurity was that of a weak manager and tied up in more personal than business issues. His behaviour was insecure, erratic, and juvenile, though he had a solid academic and professional pedigree, and the region was profitable.

My friend, was ready to get out. He decided to stay, after hearing from others that although the boss was a huge problem, HQ begged him to not leave. My friend is now positioning himself more strategically to be one step ahead of the boss, which is a lot of work, but he'll survive. He now knows who's in his corner, knows the boss' methods, and cannot only protect himself but can outshine the boss—if and only if it is necessary.

Lest anyone thinks a boss can change if given help with constructive feedback, or when coached to improve, they're wrong half the time. The boss generally doesn't think anything is terribly wrong—that's why he's in charge. Would you want to tell the person who controls your future that he's not up to standard?

This is not to say all bosses are sociopaths, but getting leaders to change their ways is generally an uphill battle. (Only when they are made aware, often through strong coaching, that they need to modify a couple of behaviours and understand the consequences of not, can change for the better occur.)

When the work situation is toxic, *and* you have fully explored your options internally, get out if there is no tangible solution. The boss will win, because he has license to push you around, and he may stay longer than you'd like to think. Line your ducks up and move when you're ready—if the option exists.

My first friend didn't simply turn in his notice. He bided his time, worked his network, and now has a couple of solid options to consider. Position yourself to build your profile internally, or go on autopilot at work and organise your time to expand externally. Either way, get moving!

Your Advisory Board

When I speak to people in transition, I often recommend they consider making their own informal advisory board.

The thinking is quite simple. If someone is thinking about what they'll do next, it's unfamiliar terrain. Uncertainty often leads to a fair amount of second guessing or hesitancy. It thus makes sense to hold on to a few steady hands; those who have been in the trenches with you, know your strengths and potential, but, more important, know your character. They become confidential sounding boards: your advisory group.

When I mention this, I often hear, 'Great idea. Why didn't I think of that'? I suspect people simply don't know how to ask for help, and the higher up one goes, the less vulnerable one wants to appear.

But the larger question to all of you is, even if you're *not* in any transition now, how often do you regularly get hold of those types of people? If you're not contacting them, what's holding you back? You're losing both collective wisdom from those who care for you and making it harder on yourself to get candid counsel.

No one succeeds alone. We all need support, and the support of an 'advisory board' is not the same as that of close friends, family, the gang at work, or the boss. A group you can lean on, in confidence, allows you to solicit opinions, which you're more likely to listen to and get feedback in a caring way. The cost is not monetary, and the return on investment (ROI) can be significant.

If you don't have such a group, start one. And if you did have one right now, what would the members likely be saying to you?

Coaching for Greatness

Another way to receive the guidance you need to take your career to the next level is through coaching.

I received a phone call from a senior software exec who got a promotion and pay raise to run a sales division—that's what he likes to do. The promotion came from his old boss in the United States. The new boss in Asia didn't seem as keen to let him run the division and wanted to get more involved with the day-to-day work than my friend wants.

But he does not know how to work his relationship with his new boss. Every time I ask what he's doing to build his rapport and credibility, he chuckles and responds that he's been so busy he has not had time to think about it. His back-up plan? Look through industry ads, send his CV back to places in the United States, and have telephone calls with them.

He is on the edge of having a latent crisis in work, but doesn't see it. I suggested he use his old boss strategically before he makes his case to his new boss. He said that sounded like a good idea and thanked me for confirming what he thought he should be doing.

He could use some one-on-one coaching now, but he won't seek it. He'll soldier on for a while, but he has no idea how tightly wound he is.

Coaching can peel the feelings to get at the core of what is holding you back. No one in a company cares much about 'feelings', and that is not what employees are paid for. But it is precisely at that moment when coaches can help—if you let them. That last *if* is a big factor.

I met with someone a while ago to determine whether he wanted coaching and for him to eyeball me. He came out swinging. A Hobson's choice in a way, as his boss had instructed that we meet. He is a senior exec with a regional role, many years' work experience, and quite knowledge-able in his business. Here's the gist of that conversation:

'I am not happy with my boss, to be perfectly honest. My wife said she thinks he's holding me back. I agree. I should be empowered more than I am'.

'Holding you back how'?

'He's critical of the way I work, and I don't happen to agree with his assessment'.

'Which is why we're here now, no'?

'He said I'm arrogant. Do I look as though I'm arrogant'?

'Explain, please'.

'Here's one example he gave. When I walk through the office I don't say hello or talk to anyone. He, on the other hand, speaks to *everyone*. He's imposing his values on me. I am not him'.

'Do you stop and chat with others when you take those office walks'?

'No, usually not'.

'Why not'?

'I'm thinking. That is how I work. I have a lot on my mind, and, quite honestly, I don't think the chitchat much matters'.

'So he's right'?

'I'm not him, am I'?

'Understood, but is he right if he says you generally don't engage in small talk with your staff'?

'Of *course* I do sometimes. I'm not a machine. But I'm there to work, not spend my time bullshitting. So yes, if that is how you define it, then, yes, he might well interpret it as arrogance'.

'But does your staff also think that'?

'I really don't know, I've never asked if they think I'm arrogant. Maybe. Does that really matter'?

'That's a telling answer. What do you think'?

'Okay, I'll ask them then'.

'Why so defensive'?

'I am who I am. It's worked okay so far. I haven't done too badly'.

'True. *The point of this is to fine tune your behaviour so you can do your job better* [my italics]. Think you should scale it back a bit when you walk through the office next time'?

'And be more like my boss'?

'No, always be yourself. But slow it down. Others may want some attention. You're dealing with your staff. They all watch you. You're judged by your behaviour, not how hard you're thinking. Act a bit differently and see how they react'.

'Oh, he also said I can be abrasive, along with being arrogant. Nice, eh'?

'And'?

'Actually, I can be, but that's my nature. I call it as I see it, which can be abrasive sometimes. I do agree with that, but I don't think that's a character flaw, just being honest'.

'So you equate abrasiveness with honesty'?

'Sometimes, I guess'.

'So . . . abrasive and arrogant is what he's told you to work on'?

'Yes'.

'You agree with the labels'?

'I can see how I might be viewed that way'.

We wrapped up that first meeting after about ninety minutes. He turned to me as we were getting ready to leave and said point-blank (with just a hint of a smile), 'So, can you save me'? He was dead serious.

Not sure I'd call it an 'aha' moment, but for a first coaching meeting, it was a breakthrough. My answer was an unreserved 'Yes', although in the end he has to save himself, I only hold up a mirror. But he was smart enough to listen, and wanted to change. The rest is gravy.

10

WHERE DO YOU STAND?

One of the most critical, yet vexing, challenges at work is to determine exactly where you rank within the company. You may think you're doing well because you hit your numbers, or that you've got a great way with peers/subordinates/clients, or simply from riding an economic wave. Conversely, you may think that one slip has labelled you irreparably.

Either way, bench-marking yourself against others may be unclear, because no one is being clear with you. If you're a superstar, you usually know it, but for the majority who are good or extremely good, along with others on the margins, you may not know exactly where you stand. Put another way, you may not be sure how to manage your own career strategy. Since you can't manage what you can't measure, the end result is a lot of jockeying, idle chatter, sharp elbows, and unpredictable morale.

Each of us must take ownership of our careers, and steer it the way we want, not outsource it to anyone else. Manage your career as if it was your life, because it is.

Whether you think so or not, you are likely facing transitions of business, which necessitate more thought. Transitions of:

- New job in the same company
- New job in a new company

- Same job, new boss
- Same company, new location
- Downsizing, but staying with the same company
- Downsizing, but no one's talking
- Rapid growth, but no one's talking
- Reorganising, which could mean anything
- Acquisition of your company (or vice versa)

You can add your variations to the theme, but the point is that work is never static, never. It is always in motion, and you have to understand how to move, how to transition, and do so proactively, not reactively. That is what separates someone who might be labelled 'savvy' from someone viewed as 'jittery'.

Life offers no guarantees, so why would anyone think a company can guarantee security? It might be easier to think the company will take care of you if you work hard. However, hard work is a contributing, but insufficient, component for peace of mind.

Andy Grove of Intel wrote a book years ago titled *Only the Paranoid Survive*.[17] He was writing about the cutthroat Silicon Valley innovators and how to maintain an edge. But part of business savvy is a healthy dollop of paranoia, just enough to keep you from complacency.

Whatever you are facing now in your career, think about your next step, in addition to the step after. Be more gimlet-eyed about what and who surrounds you. Can you make things work to your advantage? If not, how do you fix it, and with whom? A quick exit? A slow one? Not at all? Who are you turning to for counsel, with whom do you gripe? Whom do you need to get in front of, inside and outside the company, and what are you doing about it?

I went to a *New York Times* talk the other day, moderated by Tom Friedman. The subject was the 'global future', which could have kept people on the dais for years, but fortunately it was only one day. Among the comments whizzing by was how to take ownership of your career, and

---

[17]   Andy Grove, *Only the Paranoid Survive* (New York: Doubleday, 1996).

in Friedman's words, *'think both like an immigrant and an artisan'*. Take risks; you'll need to, again and again. Craft your career in a bespoke way. Your uniqueness is your value-add.

The talk of managing oneself, or managing one's career, seems almost simplistic or naïve. But it's not. In a world where many will work past the usual retirement age, with change that will whipsaw us all, it is imperative to think and act like the CEO of your own career.

Some people transition much better from one career stage to the next. What do they do differently? These people are *always* thinking ahead. They're planning three to five years down the road about how to execute their plans. Speak to any corporate CEOs and they're likely to tell you precisely what they'll be working on, and when, during the next twenty-four months or beyond. They *have* to think that way or they're toast.

Those who struggle mightily with transitioning are often mired in the work of today and tomorrow, not in future thinking. Speak to them of next steps, and the likely answer will be vague, 'working hard to make sure I'm safe', to 'being happy', or 'making sure the kids get into the right school'. All important, but these are not organised goals for themselves.

The shift from an employer managing your career to managing it yourself can cause some to lose bowel control. But this is the world we live in. It's exhilarating and liberating if you allow it to be. The ease of technology gives unbridled latitude to investigate industries, companies, people, profitability, contacts, connections, introductions, platforms, and marketplaces—all at your fingertips.

Want to transition and create your path? Think like a CEO. Know your strengths, your markets, your PR, your competition, your budget, and what your realistic future plans are. Be comfortable with not knowing if it will work exactly. The important part is to *do it*, not think it over.

I had coffee with someone reaching early retirement. Too young to stop working, but financially comfortable not to work, he was stuck. His family was telling him to relax and play golf, his colleagues were wishing him well, but he had no intention of stopping. He felt he was in his prime. A company man, he'd never had to look for a job, and now faced with the prospect of doing so, had no clue how to do it.

Start thinking about the next opportunity now—today—not tomorrow. Get hold of people you have not been in touch with and reacquaint yourself. Contact those who have helped you throughout the years to thank them—better late than never. A genuine gesture of thanks knows no time limit.

Move slightly out of your comfort zone and think (to yourself only) of doing something you would truly enjoy, which is different than what you're doing now. Chew it over, see how it feels.

I'm not saying to give up your career and go bungee-jumping. Where do you envision yourself when you daydream? Match where your skills and your heart lies, and get moving. We are all judged by our actions, not our thoughts. The sooner you take action, the better you'll feel, and the better you'll be viewed. And yes, it works.

You are your own business, no one else's. Do not expect an organisation to guide you anymore. It will not happen. That's good news and allows you to segue to the next stage of your career, in full control and in one piece.

Another case study: A friend called. The reorganising his company started two years ago finally hit him. He'd been with them twelve years in senior global roles, twenty-five years of professional experience, sterling academic, work, and legal credentials, cross-culturally sharp.

He called to see if I knew of anything in the market. He'd spent scant time building his alliances with people inside or outside the organisation, and when we talked I could hear how tentative he sounded. To be fair, he called shortly after he'd been given his marching papers, so he may have been a bit overwhelmed. But he'd seen this coming a while ago, and he hadn't done much about it, just brushed up his CV and kept working hard.

I told him to first not waste much time with *any* recruiter, and instead direct his effort reigniting his dialogue with present and past colleagues, clients, and partners, all of whom would know his strengths and competencies.

He had done what many execs do: dug himself deep in 'the job', and buried both his visibility and friendships. He'd reached a point where he didn't quite know which way to turn next, with fewer people to lean on than he should have had.

My friend is not unique by any means. Many take 'the job' more seriously than anything else. Jobs—especially today—are not permanent. Nothing is—except the old saw of death and taxes. And maybe Robert Mugabe.

Take your job seriously, of course, but remember you're only passing through. Spend time on *yourself,* not just the job. Develop your name, grow your relationships, let others know how you can help, prudently give of yourself, and *always* be aware of what's happening in the market, in part by keeping your contacts well-oiled.

The Muhammad Ali-esque 'float like a butterfly, sting like a bee' phrase makes commercial and personal sense. Keep in shape, stay light on your feet, let others know you move with grace, can take a punch, and keep moving, and that you can deliver on target.

Moments of Realisation

Opportunities will always come your way; challenges also. But the opportunities are harder to see, as they're often disguised. The million-dollar question is how to decipher what is worthwhile or not.

Some people have better antennae than others, but opportunity seldom is in flashing neon signs of 'The Big Deal'. If it is, look out. Often the best opportunity is more innocuous—an idea or surrounding, looked at from a slightly different angle.

All big ideas start off as smaller ones and compound from there. Can you see what is around you and try not to quickly categorise or shrug it off? If life is in the details, where are the opportunities?

I thought of such moments of realisation when I watched an interview on YouTube with the late Steve Goodman who died in his mid-thirties from leukaemia, and I suspect lived much more vividly than most of us. Goodman is most well-known for having written the song 'City of New Orleans'. The interviewer asked him how he wrote that song, and he said he and his wife took the train, named *City of New Orleans*, to visit her grandmother:

> '*Nancy [his wife] fell asleep, I looked out the window and wrote down some stuff, and it rhymed. Didn't take too much more than that, about half an hour. Sometimes you get visited by songs. You don't have anything to do with them, they just sort of show up*'.[18]

I love it. Sometimes you get visited by songs.

We all do, whether we have the artistry or insight to know we're being visited. They may not come perfectly, or all the time, but they show up. And when they do, capture them, and try not to forget.

Steve Goodman was a *rara avis*, one who could write a classic in thirty minutes, who knew how to capture and paint the moment.

We're all capable of doing the same thing. Don't look down or straight ahead all the time. Those moments may well be on your shoulder or outside the window, very often much closer to you than you think.

---

[18] Steve Goodman, interviewed by Bobby Bare, http://youtu.be/0F1qMgJEIbc.

11

THE RICH LIFE

In closing, a few words by Golda Meir:

> *'It isn't really important to decide when you are very young just exactly what you want to become when you grow up.*
>
> *It is much more important to decide on the way you want to live.*
>
> *If you are going to be honest with yourself and honest with your friends, if you are going to get involved in causes which are good for others, not only for yourselves, then it seems to me that that is sufficient, and maybe what you will be is only a matter of chance.*

I came across this quote the other day. I am now grappling with two teenagers soon to be college bound, so her words resonated. They are now going through the pre-university mill, asked to declare their academic interests, their gifts to society, and parrot nonsensical loops so their elders will sagely nod.

The point of her comment is simple: get *involved* with others. This is true for both young and old.

A cause—any cause—elevates people to a different level. It exposes us to a different part of life, that of giving, which we're supposed to do anyhow. Giving is always better than receiving, but oh, how easily we lose track, concerned about our private universe rather than that of others.

Get involved in something bigger than yourself! We live in a virtual world, and while the Internet connects us in new and supportive ways, we're still human. We must remain engaged to make the world better. That's the goal. Every generation is supposed to leave the world a better place, though it's easy to think we're not doing a sterling job of it these days.

Get away from the smart phone, tablet, and social media; spend time with a real community and cause. Losing sight of doing so makes us all the poorer.

What Meir didn't directly say is that you become what you do. Aristotle wrote that long ago. Virtue is indeed a habit. If we do something long enough, it transforms us. We become what we were not. Hence, patience is a virtue.

Get involved with others to raise society. Your life will take shape around that. It raises your moral game to think of others first. That's the rich life, and one well lived.

No time to get involved with life outside of work? Learn how to subtract, to let go, delegate, outsource, and reduce. Eliminate to become stronger.

This is not meant to be counterintuitive, Buddha-like advice to find a mantra, but rather a reminder that we can *all* subtract certain things and 'clean out the clutter' to improve our lives.

We all aspire to be better than we are, more charming, knowledgeable, efficient, and respected. In bettering ourselves, many of us will try to up our games with on-going education, strategic training and workshops, professional certification, or simply running a race faster, all self-improvement steps to gain new insights or capabilities. With more goals, objectives, project deadlines, targets, and profitability, the to-do list adds up quickly.

But think about the following:

Want to lose weight? You have to add exercise and *subtract* some of what you eat. Exercise alone won't do it; reducing your intake also achieves results.

Want to stop antagonising people at work or at home? Subtract the argumentative part of your conversations, and add (at a minimum) more neutral or supportive comments.

Want to stop being labelled a micromanager? Subtract the 'only I know how to do it correctly' behaviour, and add more time advising others how to do it without you, and then let them.

Want to stop being called wishy-washy? Subtract the 'I'm not sure I can . . . ', 'Do you really think this is alright to do'? and other ready-made excuses from your conversation. Stop being hesitatingly defensive. Listening and acknowledging is plenty to start redefining yourself.

Want to stop scaring people with your scowl? Subtract the facial contractions, and close your mouth more often.

Do you have projects/clients/staff/deadlines that are draining and not likely going to move the needle for you, ones you won't get credit for, potentially explosive, or a money pit? Think about subtracting them.

In jazz, knowing what *not* to play and how to use musical space is a sign of a true artist, usually accomplished after decades of playing . . . Less can be better as you progress in your career. And less can be beneficial for the other non-work realms of your life too. Once you learn how to subtract, only then can you add. Carefully.

Parting Words to Guide Your Work

Do what you have to do first, and then do what you like to do.

Adjust your goals to fit your talents and limitations so that reduced goals don't frustrate you.

Know how to proportion the means to an end, so that you don't fire a cannon to kill a caterpillar, or wave a red flag to repel a wild bull.

Recognise that others can always see you better than you see yourself. You always learn more from your critics than your friends.

Accept the fact that if you don't know how to take orders, you're not competent to give them.

Give up blaming others, and then giving up blaming yourself.

Understand the difference between pleasure, a state of having, and joy, a state of being. Pleasure fades; joy refreshes.

Know how to be serious without being solemn, and funny without being foolish.

Learn how to find more satisfaction in what you have given than what you have gotten.

'The pursuit of happiness' should be reversed to read 'the happiness of pursuit' as there is more pleasure to be found in the quest than in the goal.

Ambiguity has its advantages; better to be vaguely right than precisely wrong.

When we tell ourselves we are choosing the 'lesser of two evils', we invariably choose the easier one.

It is impossible for others to respect you if you lack basic self-respect.

The three hardest tasks are neither physical nor intellectual, but moral acts; to return love for hate, to include the excluded, and to say 'I was wrong. While it is necessary to see others weaknesses as well as strengths, it is essential to admire them for their strengths more than despising them for their weaknesses.

—Courtesy Sydney Harris

THANK YOU

Thank you for reading my book. If you enjoyed it, please take a moment to leave a review.

ABOUT THE AUTHOR

Neal Horwitz is a highly respected international consultant sought after for executive searches and executive coaching.

Horwitz has worked in Asia for over twenty years, and he and his wife, Jane Horan, currently live in Singapore. Their children, Hank and Elah, are college students in the United States. This is his first book.

www.ingramcontent.com/pod-product-compliance
Lightning Source LLC
Chambersburg PA
CBHW070816180526
45168CB00002B/639